D0026049

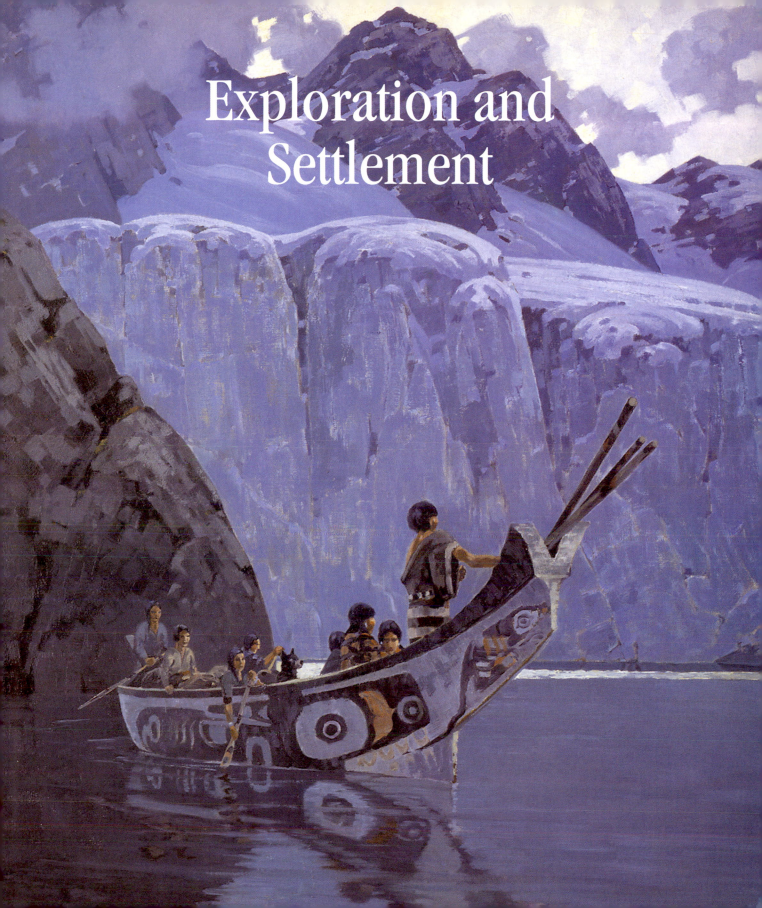

Exploration and Settlement

❧ COLONIAL LIFE ❧

Exploration and Settlement

Rebecca Stefoff

L.F. Tantillo - 1994

Sharpe Focus
an imprint of M.E. Sharpe, Inc.

Sharpe Focus
An imprint of M.E. Sharpe, Inc.
80 Business Park Drive
Armonk, NY 10504
www.mesharpe.com

ISBN: 978-0-7656-8108-9

Library of Congress Cataloging-in-Publication Data

Stefoff, Rebecca
  Exploration and settlement / Rebecca Stefoff.
     p. cm. — (Colonial life)
  Includes bibliographical references and index.
  ISBN 978-0-7656-8108-9 (hardcover: alk. paper)
 1. America—Discovery and exploration—Juvenile literature.
2. America—History—To 1810—Juvenile literature. 3. United
States—History—Colonial period, ca. 1600–1775—Juvenile literature.
4. Frontier and pioneer life—United States—Juvenile literature. I. Title.

E101.S834 2007
973.1—dc22

                                        2007003960

Editor: Peter Mavrikis
Program Coordinator: Cathleen Prisco
Production Manager: Laura Brengelman
Editorial Assistant: Alison Morretta
Design: Charles Davey LLC, Book Productions

Printed in Malaysia

9 8 7 6 5 4 3 2 1

Photo and Map Credits: Cover: © Private Collection / The Bridgeman Art Library; title page: *Return of the Experiment;* Acrylic on Canvas; L.F. Tantillo, 1994; half title, page 11: Smithsonian Art Museum, Washington, DC / Art Resource, NY; page 9: Werner Forman / Art Resource, NY; page 47: © Archivo de Indias, Seville, Spain / Mithra-Index / The Bridgeman Art Library; page 66: © British Library, London, UK / © British Library Board. All Rights Reserved / The Bridgeman Art Library; page 51: © Collection of the New-York Historical Society, USA / The Bridgeman Art Library; page 10: © Musee de l'Histoire Naturelle / Archives Charmet / The Bridgeman Art Library; page 85: © Museum of the City of New York, USA / The Bridgeman Art Library; page 61: © National Portrait Gallery of Ireland, Dublin, Ireland / The Bridgeman Art Library; pages 34–35, 43, 69, 70: © Private Collection / The Bridgeman Art Library; pages 27, 38, 59: © Private Collection / The Stapleton Collection / The Bridgeman Art Library; page 41: © Royal Geographical Society, London, UK / The Bridgeman Art Library; pages 16, 54: © Service Historique de la Marine, Vincennes, France / Lauros / Giraudon / The Bridgeman Art Library; pages 82, 88: Brown Brothers; pages 8, 13, 37, 56, 81: Cartographics; page 21: Cartographic Images; page 46: After Francois-Hippolyte Lalaisse / The Bridgeman Art Library / Getty Images; pages 32, 36, 42, 53, 65, 72, 78, 84, 62–63, 76–77, back cover: Hulton Archive / Getty Images; page 14: Ira Block / National Geographic / Getty Images; page 15: James Chatters / AFP / Getty Images; pages 18–19: The Bridgeman Art Library / Getty Images; pages 22, 40: Time Life Pictures / Getty Images; pages 6–7: Walter Rawlings / Robert Harding World Imagery / Getty Images; page 75: Library of Congress; page 87: Nancy Carter / North Wind Picture Archives; pages 17, 48–49: North Wind Picture Archives; page 25: © Parks Canada; page 28: Wikimedia.

Contents ❧

Five stories tall, with twenty rooms, the cliff dwelling called Montezuma Castle was home to the Sinagua, a Southwestern people related to the Hohokam. Today it is a national monument.

CHAPTER ONE ❧
First to Reach America

NORTH AMERICA WAS BEING EXPLORED and colonized by people thousands of years before Christopher Columbus or the Pilgrims. When the first men and women set foot on the continent, they became its discoverers and settlers. Where did they come from? When did they arrive? Scientists are still answering these and many other questions about the earliest Americans. They are searching for information about how those first arrivals spread across the continents, and how they were related to the great diversity of Indian cultures and civilizations that filled the Americas many centuries later, when the Europeans arrived.

The Peopling of the Americas

When Columbus sailed to the Americas in the late fifteenth century, he thought he had reached the eastern shores of Asia, a place that Europeans called the Indies. That is why, when he met Native American people, he called them Indians—a name that most of them now accept, even though it started as a mistake. It was not long before Europeans realized that Columbus had found a part of the world that was completely unknown. But if the people living in it were not from the Indies, who were they?

Europeans let their imaginations run wild with ideas about the origin of the Indians. Some thought that the Indians were descended from ancient Romans who had wandered halfway around the world. Others said that they were the last citizens of the mythical

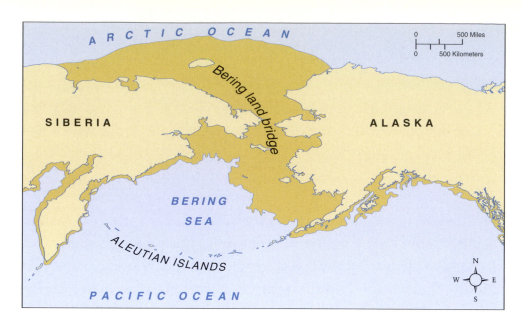

During past ice ages, when large volumes of the planet's water were tied up in great ice sheets, the level of the oceans was lower than it is today. The brown-shaded area is now covered by ocean, but it was exposed at various times during the glacial periods. The continents of Asia and North America were linked by a land bridge that animals and people could migrate across.

lost continent of Atlantis, who had fled from their sinking continent to seek refuge in the Americas. Maybe their ancestors were wandering bands of Welsh warriors, or the "lost tribes" mentioned in the Old Testament of the Bible. Eventually, these notions dropped out of scientific thinking. In their place is a new picture that is being pieced together by archaeologists, who study the physical traces left by ancient people, and anthropologists, who study people and their cultures.

Long after the human species had spread from its birthplace in Africa to Europe and Asia, the Americas remained empty of people. Then the first humans arrived. They came from northern Asia, probably from the region now called Siberia, as most modern scientists agree. But there is less agreement about when they came, and how they traveled.

By the 1970s, scientists thought they had figured out the story of the peopling of the Americas. Evidence such as stone spear points embedded in the bones of butchered mammoths proved that humans had lived in various places in North America around 11,500 years ago. Scientists gave the name "Clovis culture" to the people who made the spear points, because their type of tool was first found at a site near Clovis, New Mexico.

The age of the Clovis artifacts fits neatly together with another piece of the picture, this one drawn from the earth sciences. As anyone who has ever studied a globe or an atlas of world maps knows, Asia and the Americas almost touch in the far north. There the eastern edge of Siberia is separated from the western edge of Alaska by a stretch of water called the Bering Strait.

At its narrowest point, the Bering Strait is just 53 miles (85 kilometers) across. But during the most recent Ice Age, when periods of glaciation locked up much of the earth's water in great sheets of ice across the continents, sea levels around the globe were as much as 300 feet (90 meters) lower than they are today. Instead of being separated by water, Siberia and Alaska were linked by a broad belt of dry, open terrain called the Bering land bridge.

Scientists now know that the ice sheets formed and melted and then formed again several times between 75,000 and 25,000 years ago. As they did so, the land bridge was revealed, then covered by water, then exposed once more. The last major glaciation lasted from 25,000 to about 10,000 years ago. During that time, the land bridge remained open. Animals and people could walk from Asia to North America. So it seemed to scientists that people must have come to the Americas by crossing the land bridge, maybe following herds of the animals they hunted. They probably arrived between 15,000 and 12,000 years ago.

How did the Ice Age migrants spread southward from Alaska if the land was covered with glaciers? Geologists who study the earth and its history know that two masses of ice covered most of Canada and the northern part of the United States until about 10,000 years ago. A narrow, ice-free corridor, however, ran between these ice masses on the eastern side of the Rocky Mountains. For the Ice Age colonists of

A 10,000-year-old spear point found at Folsom, New Mexico. Workers digging up bison bones at Folsom in the 1920s found the first Folsom artifacts. A few years later, stone tools made by the people of the Clovis culture turned up farther south.

Woolly mammoths, extinct relatives of modern elephants, roamed northern Eurasia and North America during the last Ice Age. Stone weapons wielded by early American hunters have been found in mammoth bones.

North America, this corridor was a highway leading south. Eventually, the wanderers spread out and occupied all of the Americas, from the snowbound Arctic shores of North America, through the tropical jungles of Central America and the Amazon, to the deserts and mountains at the tip of South America.

Many archaeologists and anthropologists still think that is how the Americas were populated. In recent years, though, new evidence and ideas have stirred up debate. At Monte Verde, a site in the South American nation of Chile, archaeologists have found remains of shelters made of poles and animal skins that date from about 12,500 years ago, a thousand years earlier than the Clovis sites. Could people have migrated so far south from Alaska in just a few thousand years? Other archaeological digs, such as that at Meadowcroft in Pennsylvania, have led a growing number of researchers to think that humans were in the Americas much earlier than they had thought before—perhaps as many as 25,000 to 40,000 years ago. But because the evidence from these sites is not fully reliable or accepted, stronger evidence from more sites is needed to settle the question of how long people have been in the Americas.

Another new question concerns the ice-free corridor. Some geologists who have studied boulder deposits and other glacial remains now claim that the corridor was closed by ice until 12,000 years ago. If this was so, how did the Clovis people manage to become well established in the southern part of the United States by 11,500 years ago? Only more geological and archaeological research will solve the mysteries of the ice-free corridor. Yet scientists are also examining a new idea about how people might have migrated south without needing a corridor.

A band of underwater seaweed forests runs along the Pacific coast of the Americas. Forests of this towering seaweed, called kelp, are also found in Japan and around the Aleutian (eh-LOO-shan) Islands, which stretch from southwestern Alaska toward Asia. During the Ice

Artist Belmore Brown created this image of a canoe that might have belonged to the chieftain of a Native American community in the Pacific Northwest.

Age, kelp forests probably bordered the Bering land bridge, too. Kelp forests are a big help to people traveling in small boats, because the masses of seaweed can make rough waters calmer. They also provide food by attracting fish, sea birds, and sea mammals. Boat-using people from Japan or Siberia might have been able to cross from Asia to the Americas by following the "kelp highway." They could have continued down the Pacific coast, sheltering in pockets of ice-free land at the edge of the glaciers. Then, once they were south of the ice sheets, they were free to migrate inland. But proving this theory will be a challenge, because it is hard to find traces of human activity dating back to the Ice Age along the Pacific coast. When the glaciers melted, the rising seas drowned most archaeological evidence.

A Diversity of Cultures

Whenever and however they came, human beings were well established in the Americas by 10,000 B.C.E., or about 12,000 years ago. Archaeologists have coined the name Paleo-Indians (PAY-lee-o-indians), which means "ancient Indians," for these first Americans. They were the ancestors of the Native Americans, or Indians. Anthropologists have found, by comparing features such as DNA and languages, that not all Indians are descended from a single group of Asians who found their way across the Pacific. There were at least three waves of migration, maybe more.

As the Ice Age ended and the climate grew warmer, Paleo-Indian populations grew larger in many regions. They evolved into a number of distinct peoples, each with their own language and way of life. Some groups remained nomadic, moving about in search of food to hunt and gather. Others mastered agriculture, which allowed them to form settled communities. In time, large and complex civilizations

ARCTIC OCEAN

BERING SEA

INUIT

ALEUT

TLINGIT

HAIDA

TSIMSHIAN

NORTHWEST

SALISH

NOOTKA

KOOTENAI

PLATEAU

NEZ PERCE

CROW

DENE

DOGRIB

CHIPEWYAN

CREE

BLACKFOOT

ASSINIBOINE

SUBARCTIC

CHEYENNE

PAIUTE

SHOSHONE

POMO

GREAT BASIN

CALIFORNIA

YOKUT

UTE

PAPAGO

HOPI

NAVAJO

APACHE

SOUTHWEST

COCHIMI

PIMA

ZACATEC

MEXICO

TOLTEC

NAHUATL (AZTEC)

MIXTEC

ZAPOTEC

PACIFIC OCEAN

PAWNEE

GREAT PLAINS

ARAPAHO

KIOWA

COMANCHE

COAHUILTEC

OJIBWA (CHIPPEWA)

DAKOTA (SIOUX)

IOWA

SAUK

POTAWATOMI

ILLINOIS

SHAWNEE

CREE

ALGONQUIN

Hudson Bay

INUIT

NASKAPI

MONTAGNAIS

BEOTHUK

MICMAC

ABENAKI

IROQUOIS

MOHAWK

ONONDAGA

CAYUGA

SENECA

ONEIDA

DELAWARE

NARRAGANSETT

PEQUOT

SUSQUEHANNOCK

NORTHEAST

POWHATAN

TUSCARORA

CHEROKEE

CHICKASAW

SOUTHEAST

CREEK

CHOCTAW

CALUSA

SEMINOLE

LUCAYO

CIBONEY

SUB TAINO

TAINO

YUCATAN

MAYA

MISKITO

GUAYMI

CUNA

ARCTIC

ATLANTIC OCEAN

Gulf of Mexico

CARIBBEAN SEA

N
W   E
S

Agriculture
Hunting
Hunting-gathering
Fishing

0   500   1,000 Miles
0   500   1,000 Kilometers

developed among peoples such as the Olmec, Maya, and Aztec (also called Nahuatl) of Mexico and Central America, the Adena and Hopewell cultures of the Mississippi and Ohio river valleys, and the Anasazi (ah-nah-SAH-zee) of the Southwest.

Parts of the Pueblo settlement at Acoma, New Mexico, have been lived in for about 1,000 years. This church is more recent—the Spanish started building it in 1629.

No one knows how many Indians lived in North America before the Europeans came. Scholars have given a wide range of estimates, from fewer than one million people to more than 100 million. Today most researchers think that at least 5 million people, and possibly three times that many, lived north of the Rio Grande River. They formed hundreds of distinct tribes, or nations. Each tribe had its own language and way of life, but there were enough similarities among them that anthropologists can divide them into ten large clusters known as culture groups. Within each culture group, the tribes shared similar tools, customs, beliefs, and languages.

The people of the Arctic culture group, called the Inuit (IN-you-it), may have been among the last to migrate from Asia. Their skin boats, hunting techniques, and waterproof sealskin clothing are much like those of hunting peoples who still live in Siberia's far north. The subarctic tribes, such as the Dene, Cree, Algonquin (al-GON-kwin), and Naskapi, lived across Canada south of the Arctic region. They were hunting and fishing peoples. Their environment was less challenging than that of the Inuit, but they needed skill and hardiness to survive in a land where winters are long and often harsh.

The peoples of the Northwest culture group lived along the Pacific coast from the Aleutian Islands to California. Most of them were skilled seafarers who fashioned boats from skins or from cedar logs. They lived by fishing, hunting sea mammals, and gathering wild foods such as berries. Farther inland, in a climate of cold winters and hot, dry summers, lived the Plateau tribes. They hunted and gathered wild foods, and they fished in rivers such as the Snake and Columbia.

The Great Basin peoples occupied a hotter, harsher environment that included the deserts of Nevada and Utah. Here, tribes such as the Paiute, Ute, and Shoshone followed various ways of life: fishing in

The Ancient Bones of Kennewick Man ᕲ

When two college students found a skeleton in the Columbia River in 1996, they opened an unexpected window onto the early human history of North America. They also touched off a battle over the fate of the 9,300-year-old bones.

The students were wading near Kennewick (KENN-eh-wick), Washington, when they spotted a skull. Other bones soon turned up. Together, the bones made up about 80 percent of a whole skeleton that was quickly named Kennewick Man. He was not just one of the oldest skeletons ever found in North America, but also one of the most complete.

Kennewick Man fell under the control of the U.S. Army Corps of Engineers because he was found on government land. Following a law that says that Indian remains must be turned over to their tribe, the Corps planned to give Kennewick Man to a group of tribes from the region. The Indians intended to bury the bones. Eight anthropologists then filed a lawsuit to stop the bones from being turned over to the tribes. The anthropologists pointed out that there was no way to be sure that Kennewick Man was an ancestor of the modern local tribes, which developed many thousands of years after his lifetime. They also felt that the skeleton was a rare chance to make discoveries about the history that all people share.

The courts decided in favor of the scientists, who started examining Kennewick Man. They found a two-inch-long (five-centimeter-long) stone spear point embedded in his pelvis—a wound that must have been extremely painful, although it did not kill him. On his bones, they found mineral stains and other signs that his body was laid out on its back, with straight arms and legs. This means, say the scientists, that Kennewick Man was buried. Another part of their research involves making a detailed reconstruction of his facial features. This will allow people of the twenty-first century to gaze upon one of the early North Americans.

Kennewick Man as he might have looked 9,300 years ago. An artist and an anthropologist created this sculpture, based on remains found along the Columbia River.

Florida Indians, as drawn by sixteenth–century artist Theodore de Bry. Many Europeans formed their ideas about the Americas and their peoples from de Bry's pictures, which were printed in books and on maps.

lakes and rivers, hunting and gathering wild foods, and sometimes cultivating crops such as corn, squash, and melons in irrigated fields. The same is true of the California tribes; a few were farmers. Coastal peoples fished or gathered seafood such as mussels and clams. Inland tribes hunted game animals and harvested wild seeds such as pine nuts and acorns.

The Southwest peoples, such as the Pueblo and Hopi, were descended from the Anasazi and other early cultures that had built many-roomed structures in canyons and on cliff walls. They were skilled builders, and they were also highly efficient farmers who used irrigation systems to grow corn, squash, beans, and other crops in their semidesert environment. The Great Plains culture group occupied the middle of North America from Canada to Mexico. The Crow, Blackfoot, Kiowa, Comanche, and other tribes of this group were hunters who followed herds of bison across the plains.

The Southeast was home to the Cherokee, Chickasaw, Creek, and other tribes who were primarily farmers. Agriculture was also

practiced intensively in part of the Northeast. West of the Appalachian (app-ah-LAY-chyun) Mountains, however, Indians of the Northeast culture group tended to rely more heavily on hunting.

Before the arrival of Europeans,
America was an ever-changing,
dynamic world. By the fifteenth
century, for example, large civilizations such as those of the Hopewell and the Anasazi had faded
away or broken up into many sepa-
rate smaller groups. Around the
same time, the Navajo and the
Apache peoples, who came from
the Great Plains culture group,
moved into the Southwest and
adopted some practices of the
local peoples they found there.

Indians also shaped the landscape. They used fire to thin forests

so that new undergrowth would support large populations of deer to
be hunted. They cleared woodlands to plant corn, and they turned
other woodlands into orchards by planting food-bearing trees such as
hickory and chestnut.

When British settlers landed on the Atlantic coast of North America, they thought they were entering a primitive, untouched wilder-
ness, with only a few Indian inhabitants. Some historians now argue
that what the settlers really encountered was a landscape that large
Native American populations had manipulated and managed over
hundreds or even thousands of years. The arrival of Europeans
would change everything.

The native peoples of the Americas created a multitude of diverse cultures throughout the Western Hemisphere before Europeans arrived to challenge their ownership of the land.

The Viking Leif Eiriksson commanded the first European ship to reach the North American coast, according to the Norse sagas. Superb shipbuilders and seafarers, the Vikings colonized the islands of the North Atlantic Ocean.

CHAPTER TWO

The Age of Exploration

CHRISTOPHER COLUMBUS SET OUT ACROSS the Atlantic Ocean from Spain with three small wooden ships in 1492. When he returned to Europe in 1493, he opened a new chapter in the history of North America. Even before Columbus, though, a few Europeans had boldly ventured as far as the edge of North America. Some of them even set up a colony there. Later, when the desire for new trade routes spurred the nations of Europe to send navigators into the unexplored reaches of the ocean, competition between Portugal and Spain led to Columbus's world-changing voyage.

Vikings in Vinland

The Vikings discovered America by accident. The discovery was part of a long process of Viking exploration and colonization in the North Atlantic. These trading and raiding seafarers from the Scandinavian lands of Norway and Sweden were Europe's best shipbuilders and sailors in the ninth, tenth, and eleventh centuries C.E. They traveled east along the rivers of Russia and south into France, Spain, and the Mediterranean Sea. They also traveled west, island hopping across the stormy North Atlantic.

First the Vikings reached the Shetlands and the Orkneys, clusters of rocky, windswept islands north of Britain. By the beginning of the ninth century C.E., they had landed on a more distant and isolated island group, the Faeroes, about 200 miles (320 kilometers) west of the Shetlands. The Vikings established colonies in each of these island groups. Settlers fished, farmed, raised sheep, and hunted the seabirds who nested

OPPOSITE:
Ever since the Vinland map came to light in 1957, scholars and manuscript experts have debated whether it is genuine or a hoax. If it is genuine, it dates from the mid–fifteenth century C.E. and is the first map to show the North American lands visited by Leif Eiriksson— "Vinland" is the island in the upper left corner, where Baffin Island would appear on a modern map. Many experts, however, believe that the ink on this map is modern and that it was created in the twentieth century.

on the rocky crags. Through trading voyages, they maintained contact with the Scandinavian homelands.

Storms occasionally blew trading ships off course, sending them out into the North Atlantic. By the middle of the ninth century, several storm-blown Vikings had seen or landed on an island 240 miles (385 kilometers) west of the Faeroes. Late in the century, people from Norway began colonizing that island, which they called Iceland. The Norse Icelanders fished and raised sheep. Like the Faeroe Islanders, the Icelanders made frequent voyages to Scandinavia and the British Isles. They traded wool, hides, sealskins, and falcons to Norway and Ireland for grain, timber, and iron goods.

A trader named Gunnbjorn Ulfsson (GOON-byorn OOLF-son) was on his way from Norway to Iceland in the early tenth century when another fateful storm blew him off course. He was far west of Iceland when he spotted a row of rocky reefs or small islands. Ulfsson managed to turn his ship around and avoid being wrecked on the rocks, and, eventually, he made his way back to Iceland. Afterward, the Icelanders talked about the islands Ulfsson had seen, but as far as historians know, the first one to try to find them again was a fiery-tempered Icelander named Eirik the Red.

Banished from his home for three years because of violent crimes and blood feuds, Eirik led his followers west in a small fleet of ships. After a voyage of 450 miles (725 kilometers), they came to a grim, forbidding coast of ice and rock. Eirik sailed on, hoping to find habitable land. Passing a large cape, the ships followed the coast northward. Eirik was now sailing along the western shore of Greenland, the world's second-largest island (after Australia). Many geographers consider Greenland to be an outlying part of the North American continent, which is why some historians say that Eirik's voyage brought the Vikings to North America.

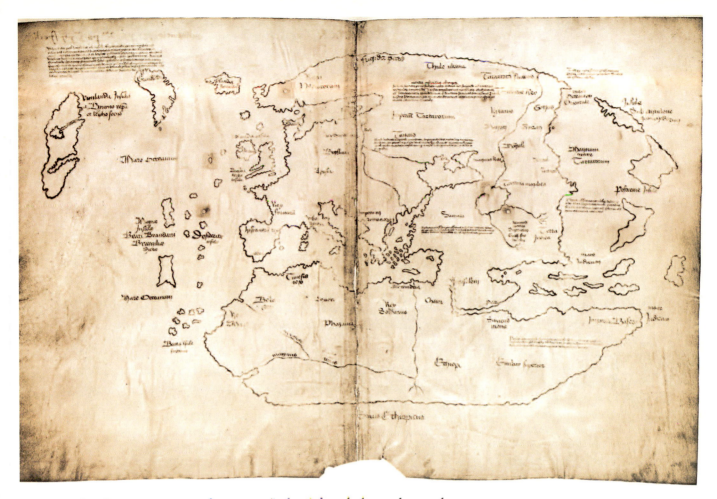

An ice cap covered most of the island, but along the west coast, Eirik located some grassy islands and inlets that were sheltered from the worst of the wind. He and his followers built huts and spent three years exploring the coast. Then they returned to Iceland and, in one of history's first great real-estate promotions, Eirik convinced a group of Icelanders to follow him back to the land he had discovered. To lure them with an attractive name, he called the place Greenland.

Twenty-five ships set out for Greenland in 982 C.E. Only fourteen ships reached their destination, but the 400 or so people they carried began homesteading along the coast. In the years that followed, others joined them. Eventually, the Greenland colony consisted of two major settlements. On the southern tip of the island was the Eastern

Settlement, and on the west coast, not far from the Arctic Circle, was the Western Settlement. Farms and homesteads dotted the coast between them. In the twelfth century the Greenlanders converted to Christianity, received a bishop, and built churches. Their land was treeless and not well suited to farming, so they were completely dependent on trade for such necessities as grain and timber. Still, for a time the Greenland colony flourished as Europe's first outpost on an American shore.

Leif Eiriksson may have sailed from Greenland to Vinland in a vessel like this one. The Norse passed down tales of his visits to North America. These legends were confirmed when modern archaeologists found ruins of a Norse colony in Canada.

The Norse who settled Greenland did not know that they had arrived and built their colony during a period of unusual weather. From the eighth through the eleventh centuries C.E., average temperatures across the North Atlantic and surrounding lands were several degrees higher than normal. With milder temperatures and longer growing seasons, Iceland and Greenland seemed to welcome settlers during this period. Then, in the twelfth century, temperatures gradually lowered to their usual level—and kept falling. Around the beginning of the thirteenth century, colder-than-normal temperatures plunged the North Atlantic region into what scientists and historians call the Little Ice Age. Winters grew longer and colder. Summers were shorter, wetter, and cooler. Life was hard across Europe, but for people in Greenland, it became agonizingly difficult.

Ice spread across the northern seas, making voyages more hazardous. At the same time, mainland Europe suffered repeated epi-

The Saga of the First Sighting ∽

The first Viking to see the North American mainland was Bjarni Herjolfsson (BYAR-nee-HARE-yolf-son). According to *The Greenlanders' Saga*, Herjolfsson was an Icelander who went on a trading voyage to Norway. When he returned to Iceland, he was surprised to find that his father had moved to Greenland. Herjolfsson decided to follow. "Our decision will appear foolhardy," he told his men, "since no one of us has entered the Greenland Sea."

Lost in fog for many days, Herjolfsson and his men had no idea which way they were going. When the fog lifted they saw low hills covered with forest. This did not match the descriptions of Greenland that Herjolfsson had heard, so he kept sailing. Two days later they sighted a flat, wooded shore. It did not look like Greenland, either, so Herjolfsson sailed on. Three days after that they spied a mountainous, icy coast. Herjolfsson refused to go ashore, saying, "For to me this land looks good for nothing." He turned his ship out to sea, and four days later they came to another shore. "This is very like what I am told about Greenland," Herjolfsson said, "and here we will make for the land."

Herjolfsson had finally reached Greenland, where he was reunited with his father and told everyone about the unknown shores he had sighted. This talk inspired another Greenlander, Leif Eiriksson, to buy Herjolfsson's ship and sail west—and the rest is Vinland history.

demics of bubonic plague, called the Black Death in the Middle Ages. The attention of Europeans shifted away from the distant Greenland colony. Trading voyages became fewer and fewer. After the late fifteenth century no one came to Greenland for many years. As glaciers crept toward the coast and crops failed, the Greenlanders abandoned the Western Settlement. They also came into conflict with the native Inuit people, whom they called Skraelings (SKRY-lings). Lacking timber or iron to repair their old broken ships or build new ones, the Greenlanders did their best to survive, but when an Icelander's ship was blown off course and landed in the Eastern Settlement in 1540, he found the settlement empty except for a single corpse. The Greenlanders had died out.

Long before the Greenland colony faded away, a few Greenlanders sailed west to the North American mainland. Old stories said that they even built a short-lived outpost there, in a place they named Vinland. And although archaeologists and historians are still debating just where Vinland was located, they have found proof that the Vikings really were the first Europeans known to have set foot on the continental mainland.

The earliest sources of information about the voyages to Vinland are two sagas, long poems that record the deeds of the Norse Vikings. *The Saga of Eirik the Red* was probably first written down sometime in the fourteenth century. *The Greenlanders' Saga* might have been written a bit before that. Both of them claim to report events that happened centuries earlier, around 1000 C.E. They tell how Leif Eiriksson, the son of Eirik the Red, led an expedition to explore an unknown coast west of Greenland.

From Eirik's homestead Brattahlid, in the Eastern Settlement, Leif and his men sailed northwest. They came to a rugged, icy shore that Leif named Helluland, meaning the Land of Flat Stones. Sailing southward, they reached a flat, wooded coast. Leif called this place Markland, or Forest Land. Still farther south, they came to a land of hills, streams, trees, and fruit. Leif called this place Vinland, or Wine Land. He and his men built houses and spent the winter there before returning to Greenland.

The sagas say that the Greenlanders made a few more trips to Vinland after Leif's voyage. Details are unclear, but the Greenlanders may have tried several times to establish permanent settlements in Vinland. They did not last. Fights with the Skraelings broke out, and

this might have discouraged the Norse from staying. Still, in the years that followed, the Greenlanders occasionally sailed to Markland, and maybe on to Vinland, to harvest timber—until their ships failed.

Most modern historians now think that Markland was probably the coast of what is now called Labrador, a large peninsula in eastern Canada. Helluland could have been the coast of Baffin Island, north of Labrador. And Vinland was probably Newfoundland, a large island close to Canada's southeastern coast. In 1960, Norwegian archaeologists unearthed a Norse settlement at a site called L'Anse aux Meadows on a peninsula at Newfoundland's northern tip. The site, which dates from about 1000 C.E., contains the remains of at least eight buildings. Researchers think that it was a temporary or seasonal camp, used for repairing ships and possibly for storing goods, such as furs and timber. L'Anse aux Meadows also may have been a starting point for voyages west into the St. Lawrence River or

No one knows for certain whether L'Anse aux Meadows was the site that Leif Eiriksson called Vinland, but the remains of these Norse buildings in Newfoundland, Canada, prove that the Vikings came to North America 1,000 years ago.

south along the coast of Maine. The camp did not remain in use for long, however, and no other authentic Viking sites have yet come to light on Newfoundland or anywhere else in North America.

Into Atlantic Waters

Between 1000 and 1500 C.E., European authorities such as the church, the Norwegian government, and various trading companies mentioned the Greenland colony from time to time in the records they kept. These records say almost nothing about Vinland and the other places Leif Eiriksson had explored west of Greenland. Yet "Leif's lands," as the sagas called them, may not have been entirely forgotten. They lived on in the Norse sagas, which were known to a few well-read people outside Scandinavia. Stories of Vinland and other western lands also might have filtered into the sea lore of sailors, fishermen, and traders who worked in the Atlantic.

Trade routes continued to link England, Scotland, Scandinavia, and Germany with Ireland, the Faeroes, and Iceland during the late Middle Ages. But Europeans had another reason for venturing out into the Atlantic: They went in search of fish.

For a long time fishing vessels had plied the seas between Norway and Iceland, and north of the British Isles as well. Their main catch was cod, also known as stockfish. Cod was an extremely useful fish. It could easily be dried, salted, or smoked. These preserving methods allowed cod to be stored for long periods, then used in soups, stews, casseroles, or porridges. Because the church taught that Christians should not eat meat on Fridays or on the many other holy days in the church calendar, there was always high demand for fish, which could be eaten at such times. Preserved cod was a major item of commerce.

The Little Ice Age of the thirteenth and fourteenth centuries meant trouble for the cod-fishing industry. The waters off Norway grew stormier and rougher, and the number of fish declined. As it became harder to catch fish in the traditional places, fishermen from Britain, Portugal, and other nations looked for new fishing grounds in the western Atlantic. They found an abundance of cod in the banks, or areas of shallow water, off the coasts of Newfoundland and Nova Scotia in what is now Canada.

As they filled their nets on the banks, these experienced sailors and fishermen may have known that they were not far from land. The presence of flocks of seabirds or the occasional appearance of fresh

A nineteenth-century artist's vision of a fishing camp in Newfoundland. Temporary camps like this one dotted the northern coast of North America in the early years of European exploration, when a demand for cod drew Europe's fishing fleets across the Atlantic.

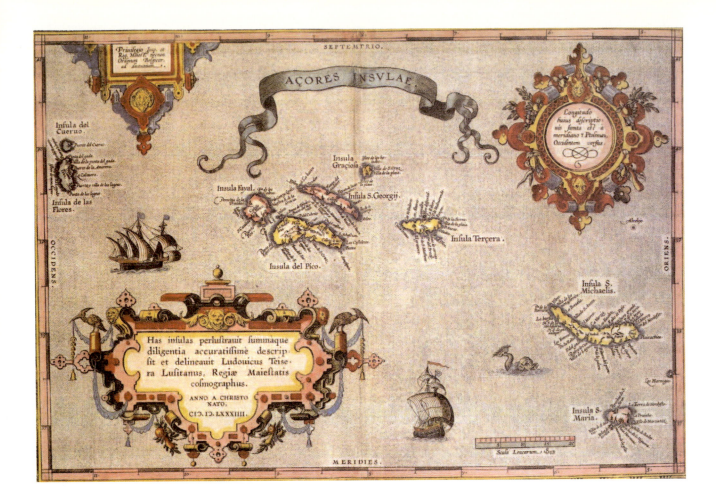

SEPTEMTRIO.

AÇORES INSVLAE.

This Portuguese map from 1584 shows the Azores Islands, one of several island groups that served as stepping-stones for European voyages into the Atlantic Ocean.

driftwood would have indicated a nearby land mass. The more venturesome fishermen—or those blown by storms—might have come close enough to the North American coast to glimpse it. Perhaps they even landed briefly to take on fresh water or to dry their catch in wood smoke. If they left no word of these landings, that could have been to keep competitors from following them to their favorite fishing grounds. There is no firm evidence that Atlantic fishermen knew of the Americas before Columbus's voyage, but it is a tantalizing possibility.

While fishermen moved into new fishing grounds in the northern waters, other voyagers were testing the waters farther south. Starting in the 1330s, captain-adventurers sailing for Spain, Portugal, and

Italy found three island groups in the eastern Atlantic. The Madeira Islands, off the coast of northwest Africa, first appeared on a European map in 1339. The following decade brought voyages to the Canary Islands, south of Madeira. The Spanish and Portuguese exterminated the native inhabitants of the Canary Islands and established orchards and vineyards there. By the 1380s, mariners had arrived in the farthest group of islands, the Azores, which lie about 800 miles (1,285 kilometers) west of Portugal.

In the course of exploring and colonizing these islands, Europeans honed their ability to navigate in the open ocean. Portuguese historians have claimed that one Azorean captain even landed in the Americas, although no evidence supports this claim. Still, those who made voyages to and around the islands learned about the Atlantic winds and currents—knowledge that would be vital to the next stage of European exploration, which was driven by the search for a sea route to Asia.

Spices, silk, gems, and other trade goods from Asia were highly prized in European markets, but the overland caravan trade with Asia was slow, hazardous, and costly. The rise of the Mongol empire in central Asia in the thirteenth century made overland travel even more uncertain. Europe's sea powers were eager to find a direct sailing route to the riches of the East.

Portugal led the way in the early fifteenth century, sending a series of navigators south along the coast of Africa. They hoped to find a route through or around that continent. When a Muslim empire ruled by the Ottoman Turks came to power in western Asia in the mid-fifteenth century, it cut off Europe's caravan trade with Asia. The search for a sea route became more urgent. Success came in the winter of 1487–1488, when Bartolomeu Dias sailed around the Cape of Good Hope at Africa's southern tip. Ten years later, Vasco da

Gama made a similar journey, but he continued all the way to India. Portugal had pioneered a route to the Indies. The next major development in world exploration would come from Spain, Portugal's neighbor and often its rival.

Spain Gambles on Columbus

Christopher Columbus's early life has some touches of mystery. In later years, Columbus's son would say that his father deliberately hid some facts about his background. Most historians, though, think that Christopher Columbus was born in 1451 in Genoa, an Italian port city that was home to many merchant sailors. He went to sea as a teenager, possibly with his brother Bartolomé, who remained Columbus's closest friend and partner throughout their lives. Later the Columbus brothers settled in Portugal, where Bartolomé worked as a mapmaker.

Columbus also did some mapmaking, but he continued to make voyages. He visited England and Ireland, and he might even have gone to Iceland, although the evidence for that voyage is slim. He also lived for a time in Madeira. Throughout these years, Columbus gathered all kinds of geographic information, from sailors' tales to the newest theories of Europe's most learned scholars.

Like other educated people of his time, Columbus knew that the world is round. He believed it would be possible to reach the East by sailing west. In other words, he planned to get to Asia by going in the opposite direction, out into the Atlantic, and sailing around the world.

There were two problems with Columbus's plan. One involved the distance of the trip. Columbus based his estimate of the size of the earth on advice from Paolo Toscanelli, one of fifteenth-century Europe's top geographers. Both Toscanelli and Columbus, however,

Columbus Reports on His Voyage ❧

While sailing back to Europe in the *Niña,* Christopher Columbus wrote a letter describing what he had found on his first voyage for Spain. The letter was addressed to a treasurer who had helped Columbus get money to pay for the voyage, but the navigator knew that the king and queen would probably read it, too.

"As I know you will be rejoiced at the glorious success that our Lord has given me in my voyage," Columbus began, "I write this to tell you how in thirty-three days I sailed to the Indies with the fleet that the illustrious King and Queen, our Sovereigns, gave me, where I discovered a great many islands, inhabited by numberless people; and of all I have taken possession for their Highnesses. . . ."

This sentence reveals a lot. It tells us that Columbus believed that the islands he saw were part of Asia, or "the Indies." He would keep up that claim for years, although there is evidence that he eventually came to realize the truth.

Columbus also felt that God had favored him with success. Other Europeans would soon share his belief that God wanted them to conquer—and Christianize—the peoples of the Americas.

Finally, the sentence ends with the statement that Columbus had "taken possession" of the islands in the name of Spain. The idea that territory was there for the taking, even though it was inhabited, would eventually bring the entire Western Hemisphere, from Alaska to Tierra del Fuego, under European control.

drastically underestimated the earth's size. Columbus thought that the eastern edge of Asia was much closer to the western edge of Europe—and therefore much easier to reach by sea—than it really is. The second problem was that, unknown to Columbus, the land masses of the Americas lay between Europe and Asia, blocking the way. When Columbus encountered these land masses, he was reluctant to accept them for what they were: continents that were not on any European map.

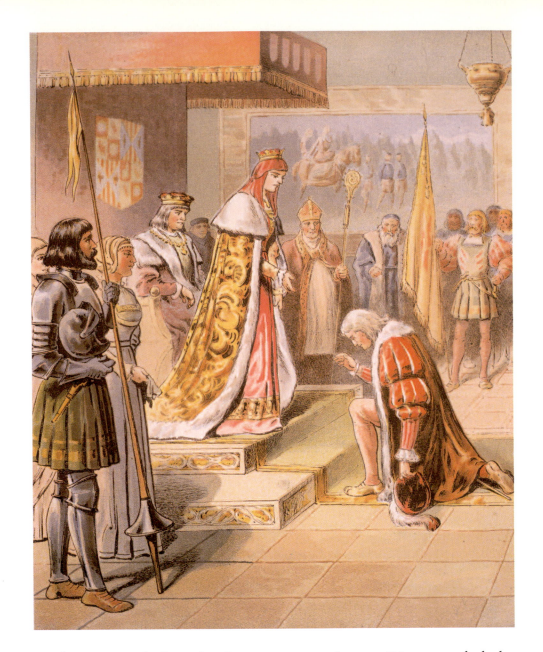

Christopher Columbus reports his great discovery to the king and queen of Spain in this illustration from 1892.

Three years before the Portuguese navigator Dias rounded the Cape of Good Hope, Columbus tried to win the support of the king of Portugal for his planned voyage. But Portugal had made a big investment in the quest for a route around Africa, and the king chose to continue with that venture rather than spend money on a voyage in a new direction. Eventually, Columbus managed to get backing from

Spain. On August 3, 1492, he set off from the Spanish port of Palos. He had three ships: the *Niña*, the *Pinta*, and his flagship, the *Santa Maria*. After a pause in the Canary Islands for fresh water, the little fleet headed out to sea and kept sailing west. On October 12, it reached land.

The location of that first landfall is not known for certain, but most historians agree that it was one of the islands of the Bahamas. There Columbus found friendly inhabitants, but none of the cities, markets, or ports that Marco Polo and other travelers to Asia had described. Figuring that he must have reached some frontier island on the edge of civilized Asia, Columbus kept looking, sailing through the Bahamas and along the west coasts of two larger islands, now called Cuba and Hispaniola. He called the people he met Indians. Some of them, he noted with great interest, wore gold jewelry. Since no Asian power appeared to be in control of these lands, Columbus claimed them for Spain—and also for himself, because the Spanish crown had promised to make him governor of any new lands that he discovered.

The *Santa Maria* ran aground on the coast of Hispaniola and had to be abandoned. In January 1493 Columbus set sail for Spain with his two remaining ships. He left about forty men behind on Hispaniola, where they had formed friendly relations with the local natives. Their assignment was to build a fort so that, when Columbus came back to the island, the beginning of a settlement would be in place. Even though he was heading back to Spain with just a small amount of gold, Columbus was confident that the king and queen, when they heard of his discoveries, would pay for a second expedition. On that expedition, Columbus wanted to do two things: locate China, India, or some other known part of Asia, and establish a profitable colony. In the end, neither of those plans would work out as he hoped.

Hernando de Soto and his band of conquistadors reach the banks of the Mississippi River. They had cut a two–year swath of destruction through the Southeast, but De Soto would soon perish in Arkansas.

CHAPTER THREE ❧
Colonies and Conquistadors

AFTER COLUMBUS SHOWED THE WAY TO

lands across the Atlantic, other Spanish navigators, adventurers, soldiers, and government administrators followed. The boldest were the conquistadors (con-KEE-stah-dors), warrior-explorers who led armed expeditions into unknown areas. Once honored as heroes, today they are more often seen as villains who destroyed a host of Native American civilizations in their search for gold and glory. Yet although the conquistadors were ambitious and often ruthless, they were undeniably brave.

Europeans were fascinated by their discovery of a part of the globe that was previously unknown to them. They called it the New World—even though it was new only to them, and not to its millions of inhabitants. Through the efforts of the conquistadors, large tracts of the New World were explored, then claimed or conquered, and finally colonized by Spain.

The First European Colonies

Columbus's first attempt to found a colony in the Americas ended in failure. When he returned to Hispaniola on his second voyage, in 1493, he found the men he had left there all dead. The fort was in ruins. Fighting had apparently broken out between the Spanish sailors and the Native Americans after the *Niña* and the *Pinta* sailed.

Abandoning that site, Columbus turned his attention to a new location farther east, where his men had discovered that the Indians possessed small amounts of gold. There he founded a settlement he called Isabella in honor of the queen of Spain, who had funded Columbus on his venture. The colonists set out to create a copy of European life in the new land. They planted seeds they had brought from Europe: wheat, beans, onions, and lettuce. They built a fort, a church, and houses, including a stone house for Columbus. He called it a palace and predicted that the king and queen of Spain would visit it one day.

Columbus had brought seventeen ships and about 1,500 people from Spain, and he soon split the expedition in two. Leaving some of the men at Isabella to collect gold from the Indians, Columbus sailed off with the others to explore Cuba. He could not make his way entirely around Cuba and did not discover that it was an island. It must, he decided, be part of the Asian mainland.

Returning to Hispaniola, Columbus discovered Isabella in disarray. The area's poor soil and lack of rain had caused the European crops to fail. The people were hungry. Many were also ill, possibly suffering from diseases such as yellow fever that were carried by the mosquitoes from nearby marshlands. Columbus decided to abandon Isabella and start a third settlement. Called Santo Domingo, the new colony was located next to a good harbor on the southern coast of Hispaniola. Some sources say that Bartolomé Columbus chose the site. If so, he chose well, because Santo Domingo endured to become the first permanent Spanish town in the Americas. Unlike the earlier settlements, it was carefully planned, with streets laid out in a grid and buildings erected in square blocks. The colonists received grants of land for ranches and farms in the countryside, but at

Christopher Columbus thought he could sail west around the world to reach the eastern edge of Asia. He would have succeeded if the unexpected Americas had not blocked his way. In four voyages, Columbus failed to find a route through them.

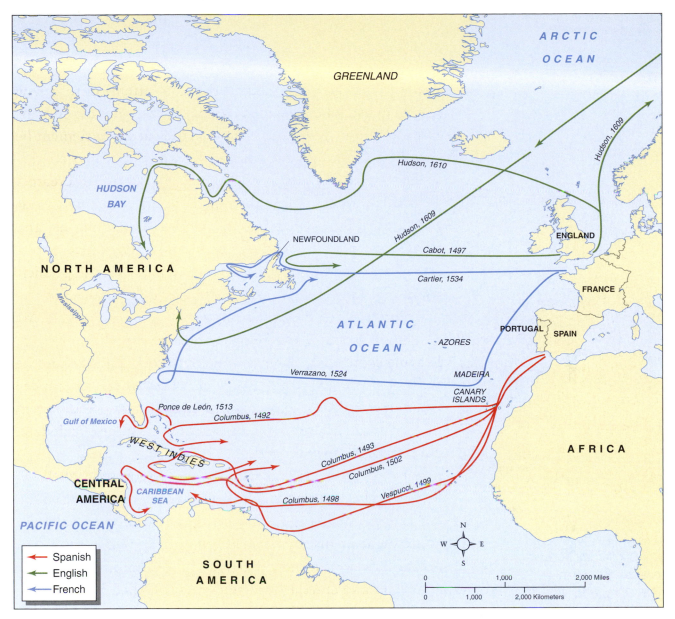

Columbus's 1492 voyage kicked off an era of exploration in the Atlantic Ocean and along the eastern coasts of the Americas, as other navigators tried to do what Columbus had failed to do: find a route to Asia.

first, most of them turned their attention to gathering gold, which they forced the Indians to provide.

By the time Santo Domingo was being built, several ships had journeyed back and forth between Hispaniola and Spain, carrying gold to Spain and bringing supplies and news back to the colony. Columbus learned that he had become the target of considerable

A man of the Carib people. The Carib lived in the northern regions of South America and the southern Caribbean when the Europeans arrived. By the end of the colonial era, only a few thousand of them remained.

criticism from enemies at court. Handing control of the colony over to Bartolomé, he went to Spain to defend himself from accusations that he was mismanaging the colony. Later, a third Columbus brother, Diego, would be placed in charge of Santo Domingo.

Columbus cleared himself in the eyes of King Ferdinand and Queen Isabella, and after several years he was granted a third expedition. It sailed in 1498. This time Columbus sailed along the coast of Venezuela, on the northern edge of South America. He recognized it as a continental land mass but hoped to find a route through it to the Indies. When he found no such route, he went back to Hispaniola, only to discover that a rebellion against him had broken out in the colony. He quelled it, but his stern measures caused some of the colonists to complain to the Spanish crown. The monarchs sent a new governor to replace Columbus and ordered the three Columbus brothers arrested and returned to Spain.

Once again, Columbus managed to save himself from disgrace. He even won royal permission for a fourth expedition in 1502. And once again, he failed to find a route to Asia. Tired, sick, and disappointed, Columbus returned to Spain in 1504. By that time, others were carrying the flag of Spain into the Caribbean and the surrounding lands. Some of them were followers of Columbus who had struck out on their own while he was clearing his name in Spain. They went south into the pearl-rich waters near Venezuela, and they also finished the exploration of the Central American coastline that Columbus had begun. One of these voyagers, Amerigo Vespucci, was among the first to declare publicly that the lands Columbus discovered were new continents. In 1507, a German mapmaker gave a version of Vespucci's first name to the New World, and the continents became the Americas.

Meanwhile, the colony on Hispaniola was growing, and by 1509 Spain had established colonies on Cuba, Jamaica, and Puerto Rico as well. From those outposts, the Spanish tried to colonize Panama, on the mainland. They established a coastal settlement called San Sebastian. Ravaged by disease and Indian attacks, however, the settlement began to fail. Then Vasco Nuñez de Balboa, a planter from Hispaniola who had stowed away on a supply ship to escape his debts, arrived in San Sebastian as a fugitive. He organized the few remaining settlers, moved them to a better location that he called Darién, and founded Spain's first permanent mainland colony, which he named Santa María la Antigua del Darién.

From Darién, Balboa conducted journeys of exploration into the interior. In 1513 he crossed the Americas at their narrowest point—the Isthmus of Panama—and reached the Pacific coast. That same year the governor of Puerto Rico, Juan Ponce de León, made the first landing in Florida, which he claimed for Spain. In the thirty years that followed, the far-ranging expeditions of other conquistadors would topple Native American civilizations and build a Spanish empire in the Americas.

The Conquistadors

When the Europeans arrived in the Americas, Mexico was home to a number of Native American peoples. The central plateau was dominated by the Aztec, who had come to power by conquering or making alliances with most of their neighbors. Aztec might, however, proved useless against the cunning generalship of a conquistador named Hernán Cortés.

Cortés was a rancher and mayor on Cuba when the governor of the colony appointed him to start a settlement on the east coast of Mexico. Cortés landed on the coast with 300 men, but soon he went far beyond the scope of his orders. Burning his ships so that his men could not turn back to Cuba, Cortés then marched into the interior. He met native peoples who lived under Aztec rule, and he cleverly took advantage of existing discontent among them to win some of them to his side. Those who joined him not only contributed local knowledge but also greatly increased his fighting force.

They marched into the interior and made their way into Tenochtitlán (teh-nohtch-tee-TLAN), the Aztec capital. There they impris-

Francisco Pizarro leads a small Spanish force in the capture of Atahualpa, the last emperor of the Inca. Before the Spanish arrived, the Inca Empire stretched over much of western South America.

oned the emperor. In 1521 after a long siege and some desperate fighting, Cortés and his followers gained control of Tenochtitlán and all Aztec territory. The conquistador renamed the capital Mexico City and set himself up as ruler of Mexico. Later, fearing that Cortés might try to turn Mexico into an independent empire, the king of Spain removed Cortés from power and placed his own officials in charge of Mexico, which became known as the colony of New Spain.

With even fewer men, Francisco Pizarro conquered an even larger empire. Pizarro was a conquistador who went into business as a miner, rancher, and slave trader in Panama. There he heard Indian rumors about a wealthy civilization to the south, on the Pacific coast. He and his partners made several voyages to Colombia, but their goal

lay farther south, in the Inca Empire that stretched for 2,000 miles (3,200 kilometers) from Ecuador through Peru and Bolivia into northern Chile.

With authorization from the Spanish crown to conquer the Inca, Pizarro sailed to the Peruvian coast in 1532. After choosing a site for a settlement, he marched inland with fewer than 200 men. Pizarro soon learned that the Inca emperor had died a few years earlier and that the empire was torn by rivalry between two of his sons. Weakened and distracted by this conflict, one of the sons, Atahualpa (ah-tah-HWAL-pah), fell under Spanish control and was eventually executed. The other son, Huascar (HWAS-car), ruled the highland city

A Dutch map from 1650 shows the Caribbean Sea and Central America. Nearly all of the American territory shown on this map was claimed by Spain.

of Cuzco in the Andes Mountains. He died and, in a series of battles, the Spanish, equipped with horses and armor, overcame a much larger number of Inca fighters. Pizarro seized Cuzco, and Peru was his. In 1535 he founded Lima, its new capital. With its mines of gold and especially silver, Peru dramatically enriched Spain. It also served as a starting point for further exploration and colonization in South America.

One of Pizarro's henchmen in Peru was a conquistador named Hernando de Soto. After the conquest of the Inca, De Soto received the crown's permission to conquer and colonize Florida—which at that time referred to everything north of Cuba. Promised governorship over a vast territory, De Soto gathered a large band of followers, who hoped to find civilizations as rich in gold and silver as the Aztec and the Inca civilizations had been.

In 1539 the expedition landed on the west coast of Florida, at what is now Tampa Bay. For the next three years, De Soto led his expedition on a long and winding path through Georgia, South Carolina, North Carolina, Tennessee, Alabama, Mississippi, and Arkansas. He used threats and force against every Native American community he entered, taking local leaders prisoner until the people had provided supplies—and, if possible, loot. Beatings, torture, and executions were common. Some Indians fought back. Others fled as the Spanish approached. Still, De Soto pushed on in his brutal quest, seeking the big payday of a gold-rich city like Tenochtitlán or Cuzco. He never found it. In 1542 he fell sick and died in

Native American rumors, and a lively imagination, led Juan Ponce de León, the Spanish governor of Cuba, on an unsuccessful search for the "fountain of youth." Legend said that the fountain's water not only preserved youth but cured all sickness.

Conquistador Francisco Vásquez de Coronado's huge expedition wanders the Southwest in search of gold, as pictured by the late-nineteenth century American artist Frederic Remington.

Arkansas. The remains of his expedition straggled through Texas and Louisiana until they reached the Gulf Coast, where they built boats and made their way to New Spain.

While De Soto was leaving a trail of destruction through the Southeast, Francisco Vásquez de Coronado was exploring the Southwest. Like De Soto, Coronado went in search of a wealthy civilization to conquer and exploit. Again, like De Soto, he failed to find one.

Coronado had come from Spain to New Spain in 1535. He was a friend of the viceroy, the royal representative in New Spain, who chose Coronado to investigate travelers' tales about cities and kingdoms that were said to lie somewhere in the unexplored region north of Mexico. In 1540 Coronado set out at the head of a huge expedition: more than 300 Spanish soldiers and more than 1,000 Indian and African slaves. They reached the pueblos, or villages, of the Zuni and Hopi people in New Mexico. Far from being gold-rich capitals, these were agricultural communities that the Spanish easily dominated. For several years, Coronado sent groups of his men on missions into Arizona, Texas, Oklahoma, and Kansas. Although they found no empires to loot and conquer, they did make an impressive, unexpected discovery—a vast, deep, brilliantly colored gash in the earth that became known as the Grand Canyon.

The Columbian Exchange

By giving Spain a claim to much of the Americas, the expeditions of Columbus and the conquistadors set the stage for the spread of Spanish colonization. Those expeditions also profoundly changed the worlds of both Europeans and Native Americans.

Historians use the term "Columbian Exchange" to sum up the biological, cultural, economic, and political effects of the meeting between Europeans and Native Americans. That meeting can be seen as a key event in human history. It led to disease epidemics on a huge scale, to an enormous transfer of mineral and agricultural resources from the Americas to Europe, and to the unwilling migration of millions of Africans to the Americas. These and other effects of the Columbian Exchange did more than shape the interactions of people during the colonial period. They molded the modern world.

On one level, the Columbian Exchange gave both Europeans and Native Americans useful new plants and animals. The Europeans introduced horses, pigs, chickens, and domestic sheep to the Americas. These animals were swiftly integrated into Native American life. The Plains Indians, for example, became superb riders on horses descended from Spanish stock, and the Navajo became skilled weavers of sheep's wool.

The Europeans also introduced new crops and foodstuffs, including garlic, rice, and onions. Sugarcane, brought to the Americas by Europeans to be grown on plantations worked by slave labor, would become a major part of the colonial economy. Ships that sailed from

A Conquistador Remembers ❧

Bernal Diaz del Castillo was one of Cortés's conquistadors during the conquest of Mexico. He went on to become a governor in Guatemala, and in 1568 he started writing *The True History of the Conquest of New Spain*. Published in the seventeenth century, the book is a valuable source of firsthand information about the Aztec empire and its fall. Here Diaz describes the large, splendid, crowded Aztec capital of Tenochtitlán as it appeared to Spanish soldiers who had climbed to the top of the central pyramid:

> So we stood looking about us, for that huge and cursed temple stood so high that from it one could see over every thing very well, and we saw the three causeways which led into Mexico . . . and we saw fresh water that comes from Chapultepec which supplies the city, and we saw the bridges on the three causeways which were built at certain distances apart through which the water of the lake flowed in and out from one side to the other, and we beheld on that great lake a great multitude of canoes, some coming with supplies of food and others returning loaded with cargoes of merchandise; and we saw that from every house of that great city and of all the other cities that were built in [sic] the water it was impossible to pass from house to house, except by drawbridges which were made of wood or in canoes; and we saw in those cities . . . towers and fortresses and all gleaming white, and it was a wonderful thing to behold. . . . After having examined and considered all that we had seen we turned to look at the great market place and the crowds of people that were in it, some buying and others selling, so that the murmur and hum of their voices and words that they used could be heard more than a league off. Some of the soldiers among us who had been in many parts of the world, in Constantinople, and all over Italy, and in Rome, said that so large a market place and so full of people, and so well regulated and arranged, they had never beheld before.

the Americas to Europe carried foods that were unknown in the Eastern Hemisphere: turkeys, chili peppers, cocoa, tomatoes, corn, and potatoes. Before long, some of these foods had been adopted into the cooking styles of many Old World countries. In some places, chiefly Russia and Ireland, potatoes became a staple crop.

The Europeans who set up colonies in the Caribbean and South America started by enslaving the local Native Americans. Later they imported Africans as slaves for agricultural and mining work.

In economic terms, the Columbian Exchange enriched Europe at the expense of the Americas. Spain was the first nation to profit from its American conquests and colonies, wringing fortunes in gold and silver from Mexico and Peru. Later, agricultural products and animal skins brought wealth to the colonial powers of Europe. Although historians debate the details of how this flow of wealth affected the various levels of European society, most agree that it helped Europe establish itself at the center of world trade and politics for the next several centuries.

Disease was the first major effect of the Columbian Exchange—and the worst. Smallpox, measles, and some other illnesses that were common in Europe and Asia did not exist in the Americas. Lacking exposure to these diseases, the Indians had developed no ability to resist them. When Indians were exposed to illnesses carried by European explorers and sailors, a catastrophe resulted.

Just as various scholars have different ideas about the number of Indians living in the Americas when Columbus arrived, they also have different ways of estimating the death toll from disease. By any count, though, it was high. Millions of people died as diseases spread with terrible swiftness through whole populations. In some places, the death rate climbed to 90 percent.

The human cost of the Columbian Exchange went beyond the deaths caused by disease. Although more Indians died from imported sicknesses than from any other cause, large numbers were killed by the Europeans more directly. Some died in massacres or fights during the conquest; others perished as a result of abuse and enslavement. The first to die were the Arawak and Carib peoples of the Caribbean, followed by the native peoples of Mexico and the Central American mainland.

Bartolomé de Las Casas was a priest who went to Hispaniola in 1499. He lived like a conquistador, with Indian slaves, until a spiritual awakening in 1514 turned him into a reformer. Las Casas devoted himself to working for better treatment of the native people. In his *Brief Account of the Devastation of the Indies,* published in 1552, he declared that the Spanish set out to destroy the Indian nations and "wipe them off the earth . . . by unjustly waging cruel and bloody wars." The slaughter depopulated whole regions. Las Casas wrote, "We can estimate very surely and truthfully that in the forty years that have passed, with the infernal actions of the Christians, there have been unjustly slain more than twelve million men, women, and children. In truth, I believe without trying to deceive myself that the number of the slain is more like fifteen million."

Africa, too, was deeply affected by the Columbian Exchange. The Portuguese were taking slaves from Africa long before Columbus sailed to America, but once the nations of Europe began colonizing the Americas, the demand for slaves skyrocketed. A large-scale international slave trade developed. An accurate measure of the misery it caused is impossible, but historians believe that, by the nineteenth century, as many as 10 million Africans had been brought to the Americas as slaves. Perhaps half that many enslaved Africans died before reaching the Americas from injuries or the dreadful conditions of the slave ships. Neither the Native Americans nor the Africans had reason to be glad that Europeans had crossed the Atlantic. The Columbian Exchange affected everyone, but its principal benefits went to the Europeans.

A slave owner who became a reformer, Bartolomé de Las Casas fought for the rights of Indians in Spain's American colonies. This earned him the enmity of the Spanish conquistadors and colonists.

French explorer Samuel de Champlain battles Huron Indians in southern Ontario. The artist, like many Europeans in the early centuries of exploration and settlement, used his imagination in picturing North America. He shows palm trees growing in the Canadian forest.

CHAPTER FOUR ❧
Into North America

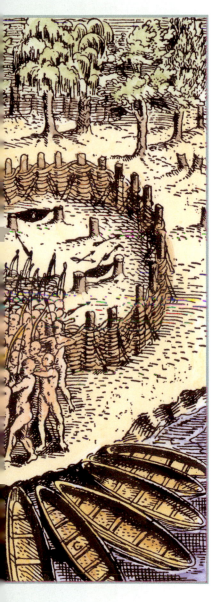

THE OTHER SEAFARING NATIONS OF

Europe did not stand idly by while Spain reaped the riches of the Americas and built a colonial empire there. Portugal was busy with its colonies in Asia, but it also established the large plantation and mining colony of Brazil in South America. England, France, and the Netherlands took a different approach. They sent navigators on a series of expeditions to probe the coastline north of the Spanish American territory. These explorers were searching for exactly what Columbus had sought—a water route to Asia.

The Elusive Northwest Passage

The Americas had blocked Columbus from finding a water route to Asia, but for a long time after Columbus, mariners kept looking for that route. For years, Spain and Portugal explored the Atlantic coastline of Central and South America, checking every bay and river mouth to see if it offered a passage through the continent. Finally, in 1520, Ferdinand Magellan made his way through the islands at the southern tip of South America and reached the Pacific Ocean, only to find that the distance to Asia was still much greater than anyone had thought.

Magellan had proved that it was possible to sail around the Americas to the south, but other navigators dreamed of finding a shorter, less hazardous route. They were sure there must be a way to sail through or around North America from the North Atlantic Ocean. This geographic fantasy came to be called the Northwest Passage.

One of the first to seek the Northwest Passage was John Cabot, born Giovanni Caboto in Italy. He became a citizen of the Italian city-state Venice, and then, in the flurry of excitement that swept across Europe after Columbus's early voyages, he went to work for England. Cabot won backing from King Henry VIII for a voyage to the region north of the area that Columbus had explored. Hoping to reach Japan, Cabot sailed in 1497 with one ship and eighteen men from Bristol, an English city that was a hub of North Atlantic shipping. After thirty-five days Cabot came to a wooded coast. He landed, did some exploring, claimed the place for England, and then sailed home.

Cabot's Discoveries ∾

On August 23, 1497, Lorenzo Pasqualigo wrote a letter to his brothers. Like John Cabot, Pasqualigo was a native of the Italian city-state of Venice who was living in England. His letter reported the news of Cabot's first voyage and the plans for his second. It ended with a note of patriotic pride for Venice, whose patron saint was St. Mark. Pasqualigo wrote:

Our Venetian [Cabot], who went with a small ship from Bristol to find new islands, has come back, and says he has discovered, 700 leagues off, the mainland of the country of the Gran Cam [the ruler of China], and that he coasted along it for 300 leagues, but did not see any person. . . . The king has promised [Cabot] for another time, ten armed ships as he desires, and has given him all the prisoners, except such as are confined for high treason, to go with him, as he has requested. . . . The English are ready to go with him and so are many of our rascals. The discoverer of these things has planted a large cross in the ground with a banner of England, and one of St. Mark, as he is a Venetian; so that our flag has been hoisted very far away.

Cabot had made the first English landfall in the Americas. The following year, he set out again with a larger expedition. Cabot was determined to reach Asia and establish a spice trade between England and the Asian markets. One of his six ships turned back to England. The others were lost with all hands, including John Cabot.

Ten years later, Cabot's son Sebastian followed in his father's wake, searching for the Northwest Passage on behalf of England. Although the younger Cabot voyaged along a great stretch of the North American coastline, from modern-day North Carolina to Labrador, he did not find the passage. After that disappointment, England lost interest in North America for about seventy years.

France was next to take up the quest to find the Northwest Passage. In 1524 King Francis I, who was the patron of many Italian artists and thinkers, granted a group of bankers and investors the right to send an Italian navigator named Giovanni da Verrazano on a voyage of exploration. Verrazano had two missions: to find the Northwest Passage and to locate lands suitable for France to colonize. Verrazano reached the coast of North Carolina. Exploring northward, he passed the mouth of Chesapeake Bay, which he named the Verrazano Sea. He thought that it could be the Northwest Passage but did not pause to investigate. After anchoring in the bay that is now New York Harbor, Verrazano continued north along the coast. In Rhode Island, he met and traded with the Wampanoag (wom-pah-NOH-ahg), whose appearance and manners he admired. Farther north, in Maine, he encountered the Abenaki. He disliked them, so he named that coast the Land of Bad People, though he praised its scenic beauty.

This seventeenth-century ceramic figure may represent Giovanni da Verrazano, an Italian navigator who explored for France. He gave the short-lived name Verrazano Sea to the body of water now known as Chesapeake Bay.

New England in California? ∾

Between 1577 and 1580, the English captain Francis Drake made a voyage around the world to pillage Spanish colonies and trade for spices. Returning to England with the hold of his ship packed full of gold, silver, and cloves, Drake became a popular hero and won a knighthood from Queen Elizabeth I.

Midway through his voyage, Drake sailed his ship, the *Golden Hind*, along much of the west coast of North America. Near what is now San Francisco Bay in California, he landed to make repairs. During the five weeks that he and his men spent there, they established friendly relations with the local Miwok. Drake claimed the land for England and called it New Albion (Albion is an old name for England). But he left no colony, and England never pressed its claim, so California came under Spanish control.

Verrazano returned to France in 1525. He hoped to make a second voyage to North America, but the king was preoccupied with war, and the bankers did not think such a voyage would be profitable. So Verrazano never returned to the Verrazano Sea or the Land of Bad People, but he did visit Brazil and the Caribbean. The latter voyage was his final journey—he was killed and eaten by Carib Indians in 1528.

By the 1530s, King Francis was ready to send another French expedition to North America. The king still wanted to find the Northwest Passage, but he was also interested in finding precious metals. He hoped for a source of wealth to match the huge fortunes that Spain was taking from its American colonies. To head the expedition, the king chose a skilled navigator named Jacques Cartier, who may have sailed with Verrazano.

Equipped with two ships and sixty-one men, Cartier crossed the North Atlantic in 1534. He landed in Newfoundland, which by that time was well known to French fisherman. Heading south to avoid sea ice, Cartier entered the Gulf of St. Lawrence. He explored part of the gulf, made contact with several Indian tribes, and—to mark a territorial claim—set up a cross inscribed "Long Live the King of France" before turning toward France. On his return, he took with him two Huron Indians, sons of a chieftain named Donnaconna. Some accounts say that Cartier kidnapped them. Others say that Donnaconna let Cartier take them so that they could learn French and serve as interpreters between the two peoples.

Cartier had found neither gold nor the Northwest Passage, but he sailed back to France with enough interesting information that King Francis I authorized a second voyage the following year. Cartier returned to the Gulf of St. Lawrence, and this time he sailed up the broad St. Lawrence River into the interior of the continent. He was sure that he had found

a navigable Northwest Passage, but that hope died when he discovered that rapids blocked the river at the site of present-day Montreal. Cartier headed back to France with detailed information about the river and the Indian towns on its banks. He had also heard stories from his interpreters about Sanguenay (sang-wen-AY), a fabulously rich kingdom that was supposed to lie farther inland. Determined that the king and court should hear those stories directly from the Indians, Cartier kidnapped Donnaconna and other tribal leaders, all of whom died in France.

Cartier was eager to find Sanguenay, but a war between France and Spain interfered with his plans for a third voyage. Finally, in 1541, he was ready to depart. His ships would carry more than a thousand colonists, some of whom were convicts. Women were included among the colonists, who were supposed to build a settlement and

Jacques Cartier, a skilled navigator, was one of several explorers who believed he had found gold or diamonds in North America, only to discover that he had hauled home a shipload of useless rocks. For years after Cartier's voyage, people used the phrase "a Canadian diamond" to refer to something worth much less than originally thought.

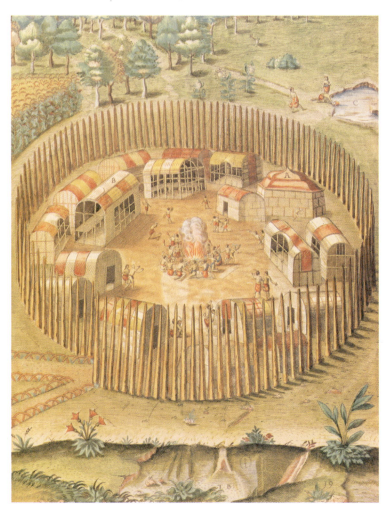

An Indian village in Florida, illustrated by Theodore de Bry in the 1580s. The poles surrounding the settlement were meant to serve as protection from attack.

establish a permanent French colony in Canada. At the last minute, Francis gave command of the expedition to one of his courtiers, a nobleman named Jean-François de la Roque de Roberval. The king demoted Cartier to navigator.

The expedition reached the St. Lawrence and chose a building site west of the present-day location of Quebec City. There Cartier established a settlement he called Charlesbourg-Royal. Few details are known about it, but records of the expedition say that Cartier ordered two forts to be built to protect the settlement. One was at the top of a cliff, the other at the bottom. Under his direction, the colonists cleared some land for planting gardens, but they probably expected to get food from the Indians, too.

To Cartier's delight, both gold and diamonds were found in the area. While the colonists went to work gathering riches and building their settlement, Cartier set off in search of Sanguenay. But he was unable to find a water route that was not blocked by waterfalls, so he returned to Charlesbourg-Royal. Things there were falling apart. The Huron had realized that the French were not simply visiting but had come to stay, and this had made the Indians hostile. Several dozen colonists had died in raids.

After an uncomfortable winter, Cartier took some of the colonists and returned to France, openly defying Roberval.

Unfortunately for Cartier, his diamonds and gold turned out to be quartz and iron pyrite (a shiny but worthless rock that is sometimes called "fool's gold"). The king authorized no further expeditions, so Cartier never returned to the search for Sanguenay, which, in fact, did not exist—it was simply a tale manufactured by the Indians. Even Charlesbourg-Royal was a failure. After Cartier left, Roberval and the rest of the colonists endured a second miserable winter. A quarter of the settlers died. The harsh climate, coupled with the fact that the settlement had earned no profit, led Roberval and the survivors to abandon Charlesbourg-Royal. They sailed back to France in June 1543. For some time afterward, French activity along the St. Lawrence River was limited to occasional trading voyages. But although Cartier's attempt to plant a permanent settlement had failed, his three voyages had produced a wealth of highly accurate geographic knowledge that would later help France turn the river into the heart of its American colony.

The Quest Continues

By the late sixteenth century, England was ready to return to North America, still with the goal of finding the Northwest Passage. Geographers had decided that the passage must lie farther north than anyone had thought. They believed that the long days of the Arctic summer would keep the polar sea from freezing, so that a safe route could exist in waters once thought to be too cold and perilous for navigation. To find the Northwest Passage, the new thinking ran, navigators should look west of Greenland, where no European had voyaged since the days of Leif Eiriksson and the Norsemen.

North America map showing European exploration routes and colonization by 1650. Labels on map include: NORTH AMERICA, ROCKY MOUNTAINS, APPALACHIAN MTS., Mississippi R., Missouri R., Ohio R., Colorado R., Rio Grande, St. Lawrence R., NEW FRANCE, Quebec, Montreal, Ft. Orange, NEW ENGLAND, Pemaquid, Salem, Boston, Plymouth, Providence, Hartford, New Haven, New Amsterdam, NEW NETHERLAND, VIRGINIA, St. Mary's, Jamestown, Santa Fe, El Paso, Saltillo, Monterrey, New Orleans, St. Augustine, NEW SPAIN, Mexico City, Havana, CUBA, HISPANIOLA, ATLANTIC OCEAN, PACIFIC OCEAN, Gulf of Mexico, CARIBBEAN SEA.

Explorer's Routes

Spanish
- De Soto (1538 – 1542)
- Coronado (1540 – 1542)

French
- Champlain (1608 – 1615)
- Joliet and Marquette (1673)
- La Salle (1679 – 1682)

Areas Colonized by 1650
- Spanish
- French
- English
- Dutch
- • Key settlements
- Modern United States border

0   500   1,000 Miles
0   500   1,000 Kilometers

During the sixteenth and seventeenth centuries, Europeans planted colonies along the edges of North America and took the first steps toward exploring the center of the continent. While the English concentrated on the Atlantic seacoast, the French approached from the north, by way of the St. Lawrence and Mississippi rivers, and the Spanish approached from their colonies to the south.

In 1576 Queen Elizabeth I sponsored a voyage of exploration by Martin Frobisher, who had captained slave ships to the Caribbean. Departing from the Shetland Islands, Frobisher passed the southern tip of Greenland and continued northwest. He came to a rocky shore, but a wide waterway entered it from the west. Here, Frobisher believed, was the long-sought Northwest Passage at last.

After an encounter with some Inuit led to the disappearance of five crewmen and a lifeboat, Frobisher decided that it would be dangerous to continue up the waterway without a bigger expedition. He returned to England. As evidence of his discoveries, he brought back a rock that he thought contained gold. He also carried a captive Inuit man and his kayak.

Queen Elizabeth provided money for voyages back to the same place in 1577 and 1578. (On one of those voyages, Frobisher stopped along the way in Greenland, where he found some long-abandoned tents but no people.) Instead of pushing farther along the westward passage he had found, Frobisher concentrated on gathering tons of the gold-bearing rocks to take back to England.

Both Frobisher's glittering rocks and his promising-looking passage were deceptions. Like Cartier's "gold," Frobisher's rocks were only iron pyrite (Canada has a plentiful supply of this mineral). The passage was later found to be a dead end. It is merely a long inlet, now called Frobisher Bay, on Baffin Island in the Canadian Arctic.

In the 1580s, John Davis, an English navigator, returned to the waters around Greenland in a series of three expeditions. South of Baffin Island, he found another channel leading west, but he did not have time to explore it. Davis also charted part of the Greenland coast, established relations with the Inuit there, and set up a fishery near the site of one of the old Norse settlements. These actions by Davis began to bring Greenland back into the awareness of Europeans.

First Footholds

Within a very short time after Columbus's return from his first voyage, fishing boats of many nations were visiting the North American coast, setting up seasonal or temporary camps, sometimes trading with the Indians. Because they had no permanent residents, these were not true settlements, although they did bring Europeans into early contact with the Native Americans of Canada and Maine.

By the end of the sixteenth century, France and England were experimenting with more formal attempts at settlement. To the south, the Spanish crown was devoting great resources of money and men to founding a vast colonial empire in the Caribbean, Mexico, and South America. The first colonizing efforts of France and England would be more modest.

France had already tried and failed once, at Charlesbourg-Royal. Then, in 1562, a group of Huguenots (HYOO-geh-nots), or French Protestants, tried to settle on the South Carolina coast, on the shore of Port Royal Sound. The Huguenots had two reasons for wanting to establish an American colony. As French citizens, they were eager to keep Spain, France's enemy, from controlling the entire American coast. As Protestants, they hoped to create a place where they could escape from the widespread religious persecution happening in Catholic France at that time.

The Huguenot settlement on Port Royal Sound remained small, but two years later another group of Huguenots built a second settlement. This one was located on the Atlantic coast of Florida. The arrival of the Huguenots infuriated Spain, which considered itself the owner of Florida. In 1565 a Spanish force led by Pedro Menéndez de Avilés wiped out the Huguenot colonies. To maintain a secure Spanish hold on the area, Menéndez turned a temporary Spanish military outpost called St. Augustine into a permanent settlement.

St. Augustine was built on a peninsula in Matanzas Bay, on Florida's Atlantic coast. The town, a collection of wooden buildings on narrow streets, was surrounded on three sides by water. The fourth side was the peninsula that connected the town with the mainland. To protect this approach, Menéndez ordered the construction of a set of defenses. A moat or ditch was cut across the peninsula to slow any attackers. Behind the moat was a palisade, or wooden wall, guarded by a fort.

The settlement's chief purpose continued to be military. St. Augustine was meant to protect Spain's claim to Florida and to serve as an

By the time this Dutch map was published in 1606, Europeans had a fairly good idea of the shape of South America. The upper reaches of North America remained a complete mystery, though, and the mapmakers had imagined a huge landmass north of South America.

army and navy base for attacks on the foreign forces that meddled in Spanish territory. For a long time after Menéndez's day, St. Augustine was a fairly unimportant outpost on the northeastern edge of Spain's American territory, but it did remain inhabited continuously. Today St. Augustine is the oldest European-built town in the United States that has been lived in ever since it was founded.

By the dawn of the seventeenth century, King Henry IV of France was eager to develop a lasting French presence in the Americas. Such ventures were costly, however. The king's solution was to offer a deal: If a person or company took the risk and established a successful colony, that individual or group would receive complete control of the trade in furs from the colony. The skins and furs of North American animals—especially beaver—were becoming very highly prized in Europe, so this offer held the possibility of great profit.

But it was not easy to create a permanent American settlement, as a geographer and mapmaker named Samuel de Champlain discovered when he tried to establish a colony in 1604–1605 in what is now Nova Scotia, Canada. Discouraged by the cold, with their ranks thinned by sickness, the colonists produced no income from furs. After the king took away their monopoly on fur trading in the area, the colonists returned to France.

The English tried, too. One of their expeditions visited the Outer Banks, a string of islands off the North Carolina coast, in 1584. Back in England, the expedition leaders reported that the islands would be a good site for a colony. Sir Walter Raleigh, one of Queen Elizabeth's courtiers, provided the money to equip an expedition to Roanoke Island in 1585. After establishing a settlement on the island, some members of the group returned to England the following year to report to Raleigh. Their verdict on Roanoke as the location for a settlement was mixed. On the one hand, it was an attractive setting. On the other, the harbor was poor, and the island was wracked by severe storms.

Raleigh paid for a second expedition in 1587. Its leader was John White, one of the colonists who had returned from Roanoke. White's colonists were bound for a site on the Chesapeake Bay, north of the Outer Banks. But during the Atlantic crossing, hostility developed between White and the ship's pilot. When the ship stopped at Roanoke on the way to the Chesapeake, the pilot forced White and the other colonists to leave the vessel. They would have to settle at Roanoke, even though the site was not to their liking.

One of the first events at Roanoke was the birth of a child to White's married daughter. The baby, named Virginia Dare, was the first English child born in the New World. Then the colonists decided that White should return to England to ask for more supplies. Before he left, he and the colonists agreed that they should move their settlement to a new location. Some of the people, though, would remain at Roanoke to await White's return. The story ends in a well-known mystery. White was delayed in returning to North America. When he finally managed to get back to Roanoke in 1590, the settlement was empty and everyone was gone. The fate of the "Lost Colony" has never been determined. The first English attempt to colonize North America had ended in failure.

Sir Walter Raleigh was the restless, adventurous spirit behind two doomed enterprises in the Americas: the lost colony of Roanoke off the Carolina coast, and the search for El Dorado, the fabled city of gold, in South America.

Jamestown, Virginia, was the first permanent English settlement in what is now the United States. It was designed to be defended from the palisade's three corners.

CHAPTER FIVE 🙰
Adventurers and Pilgrims

THE DISAPPEARANCE OF THE ROANOAKE

colony did not prevent the English from trying again to secure a foothold in North America. There was national glory to be gained by planting the flag on American soil, and England had no desire to see the New World divided between Spain and France. But another important motive for the early English attempts at colonization was money.

In 1584, while Sir Walter Raleigh tried to interest the queen and others in backing his scheme to set up a colony, his friend Richard Hakluyt, a writer and geographer, prepared a list of reasons why England should colonize America. One big reason was profit. America was rich in resources such as fish, furs, and timber. These valuable commodities would flow from the colony back to the parent country. At the same time, the colonists would depend on the parent country for manufactured goods, such as glass, cloth, and paper. English merchants would make money by selling such things in the colonies. (Hakluyt also pointed out that a colony would be a handy place to dump troublesome elements of the English population, including foolish young people, discontented former soldiers, and the children of beggars.)

The desire to win fortunes led one band of settlers to America in the early seventeenth century. Religion led another group. These two colonies ultimately endured, giving England a lasting presence in America.

The Jamestown Colony

Thirty years after Roanoke, 144 Englishmen set out in three ships to colonize Virginia. They were part of a commercial venture, a company organized to run a colony for profit. King James I had granted the company permission to settle on territory claimed by the crown.

The Virginia colonists were not very well suited to the hard work of founding a settlement. Many of them were "gentlemen adventurers," members of the upper middle class who might have served as soldiers but had no experience operating business ventures. A few were merchants or traders. Still others were the gentlemen's servants. These groups found it difficult to cooperate. In addition, pride and competition for power led to quarrels, even duels. Finally, most of the men lacked the practical skills, such as carpentry and ironworking, that would be essential to a small colony isolated thousands of miles from its parent country. By the time the expedition landed in April 1607 on a peninsula in the James River, thirty-nine of its members had died during the voyage. As the survivors started building the settlement they named Jamestown, their prospects for success were not bright.

They soon had new problems. In the years just before the English arrived, the local Native Americans, an Algonquian-speaking people known as the Powhatan after the name of their chieftain, had been on an aggressive campaign against other tribes. Through threats and war, Powhatan had won control over much of eastern Virginia. He was not happy to see the English setting themselves up in his territory. Relations between the two peoples started off with an Indian attack that killed ten colonists. Later the relationship became more peaceful—even friendly at times—but it was always uncertain.

Disease also attacked the newly arrived settlers, killing fifty of them by September. The first winter at Jamestown was extremely hard. Without the corn they received from Powhatan's people in ex-

change for such items as axes and cooking pots, all the English would have perished. As it was, only thirty-eight of them survived. However, during the following year, ships brought new colonists as well as supplies. The colony had a population of 500 by the fall of 1609.

Once again, however, winter brought disaster. Although the original plan had called for the settlers to grow their own food, they had not done so. They had not come all the way to America, they declared, to be farmers—they wanted to spend their time exploring and looking for treasure. So they relied on trade with the Indians to supply them with corn. They did not take full advantage of their opportunities to hunt and fish, either. As a result, they entered the winter of

A Dutch ship landed in Jamestown in 1619, carrying the first twenty African slaves to North America. By that time as many as one million enslaved Africans had been taken to European colonies in the Caribbean and South America.

John Smith drew the portrait of Powhatan that appears in the upper left corner of this 1622 painting. Smith had many encounters with the Indian chieftain during his time at Jamestown.

1610 with insufficient food supplies. This time, they received little aid from the Indians. Powhatan was involved in a power struggle within his tribe, and he was also displeased at the increase in the number of English settlers. Relations between Jamestown and the Native Americans had entered a hostile phase.

The settlers who survived the winter of 1609–1610 at Jamestown later called it "the starving time." Many of the colonists died. Some ran off to take their chances on life with the Indians. When a new governor arrived in Jamestown in June 1610, he found only sixty of the 500 colonists remained. They were about to give up and return to England when another ship delivered supplies and more colonists. Yet even the nightmare of the starving time was not enough to make the Jamestown colonists work to support themselves. Another new governor came to the colony in 1611. He was dismayed to find no farms and only a few private gardens. The colonists spent some of their time and energy raiding Indian villages. They passed much of the rest of the time bowling in the streets, setting up targets and trying to knock them down by rolling wooden balls at them.

The gentlemen adventurers of Jamestown had failed to find gold, silver, or anything else of value. The colony had not turned a profit. In fact, it was a constant drain of supplies and people, with nothing to show in return. King James I had tried to remedy matters in 1609 by making the governorship of the colony more like a military command, with strict rules about behavior. This change had not helped much.

What turned Jamestown's fortunes around was the discovery in 1613 of an unexpected kind of treasure. The Indians had shown the Europeans how to smoke the leaves of the tobacco plant, which was unknown in Europe. The West Indies, as the Caribbean Islands were called at this time, produced a type of tobacco that was milder—and therefore more pleasing to Europeans—than the tobacco grown by the Indians of North America. One of the Jamestown settlers, John Rolfe, introduced the mild variety of tobacco to the Virginia colony, where it grew well. Smoking was beginning to catch on in Europe, and the colonists discovered that they could sell a tobacco crop for a good price in England.

The sudden possibility of wealth filled the Jamestown colonists with energy and ambition. In the streets where they had once bowled, they planted tobacco. Within six years, the colony shipped ten tons of tobacco to England. Tobacco farming was becoming such big business that Rolfe bought twenty African slaves, marking the beginning of the slave trade in North America.

While the Jamestown colony was finding its economic footing, back in Europe another group of English men and women prepared to colonize Virginia. They were Puritans, and they did not want to come to America to seek treasure. They wanted to find a place where they could practice their religion on their own terms.

The Plymouth Colony

Puritanism was a religious movement among Protestants in England in the sixteenth and seventeenth centuries. It arose out of the complicated history of the Church of England, also called the Anglican Church. The Church of England was born when King Henry VIII withdrew England from the Roman Catholic Church because the pope would not grant him a divorce. Henry organized the Anglican Church, which adopted the Protestant variety of Christianity but did not do away with all aspects of Catholic worship.

The Anglican version of Protestantism did not satisfy people who yearned for a stricter Protestant faith. These people were called Puritans, because they wanted to reform, or purify, the church. Those who split off from the Church of England to form their own sects were called separatists—but the crown also called them traitors. To avoid trouble with the government, in 1607 some separatists fled to the Netherlands, which was known for its religious tolerance.

Despite the religious freedom they enjoyed in the Netherlands, the separatists found life there less than perfect. As foreigners, they encountered economic and social setbacks and a language barrier. They decided to build their own pure society in America, where they would

support themselves by selling their fish to England. With the help of a London merchant, they managed to get permission to establish a settlement in Virginia, with their religious freedom guaranteed. A new stock-issuing corporation, the Plymouth Company, financed the expedition. By 1620 the separatists, known as Pilgrims because they were making what they believed to be a holy pilgrimage, were ready to set sail for Virginia.

Their expedition got off to a shaky start. Delays kept them from launching until August, late in the year to begin a voyage across the stormy Atlantic. They had not gotten far when one of their two ships proved completely unseaworthy and forced them to turn back to Eng-

The nineteenth-century American artist Nathaniel Currier illustrated the landing of the Pilgrims at Plymouth Bay in December 1620. Nearly half of the Pilgrims perished in the first harsh winter that followed their arrival in North America.

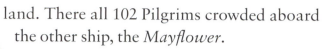

John Smith helped establish both of England's first two American colonies. A few years after he organized and briefly governed the Jamestown settlement, Smith explored and mapped the coast of New England, then published a book saying that it would be a good site for a colony. The book was a source of information for the Pilgrims at Plymouth.

land. There all 102 Pilgrims crowded aboard the other ship, the *Mayflower*.

The *Mayflower* survived the journey. It did not, however, reach its desired destination. In November the ship made landfall well north of Virginia in New England. Winter was just around the corner. The Pilgrims were poorly supplied, and most of the fishing equipment they had brought was useless. They spent a month scouting the coast, looking for a good place to build a colony—and looking even more desperately for food.

Luckily for them, they found some empty Indian houses to ransack. They found ten bushels of stored corn and carried it off. They also stole a large metal kettle that the owner of the house had clearly acquired through trade with one of the many European fishing or exploring parties that stopped along the New England coast. The Pilgrims realized that the Indian corn had saved their lives. One of them, Edward Winslow, wrote, "And sure it was God's good providence that we found this corn, for else we know not how we should have done."

As the setting for their colony, the Pilgrims chose a place they named Plymouth Bay, in what is now Massachusetts. Just a year earlier, Sir Ferdinando Gorges had tried and failed to establish an English colony there.

The Pilgrims' first winter in America was a harsh one. Almost half of them died. The following spring, the survivors received help from

Tisquantum (tih-SKWAN-toom), whom they called Squanto. He was a Wampanoag Indian who had lived in Spain and England and could speak English. He taught the Pilgrims how to grow corn and remained with them until his death in 1622.

By the time another ship sailed into Plymouth Bay in November 1621, bearing some supplies and thirty-six new settlers, the Plymouth colony had passed its greatest crisis. England now had two outposts on North America's Atlantic coast.

Colonists and Native Americans

Relations between the first English settlers and the Native Americans took many forms, from aid to aggression. Although there are reports of friendly relationships, with individual Indians and whites treating one another as equals, most interactions involved an uneven balance of power or some degree of misunderstanding.

Because the two groups were so different in their customs and goals, each side had an unclear or incomplete vision of the other. The majority of Europeans viewed the Native Americans as heathens, because they were not Christian. Europeans also referred to them as "savages," primitive people who lacked such things as horses, the wheel, writing, and guns. Native Americans, on the other hand, soon came to describe the Europeans as greedy, untrustworthy, and dirty (most Indians bathed often and were surprised that Europeans did not).

Europeans who came to the Americas often depended on help from Indians, who served as interpreters, guides, and providers of food and other necessities. Yet Europeans were often quick to exploit, or take advantage of, the Indians. One form of exploitation that occurred over and over again was the seizure of natives who were taken back to Europe. Sometimes these luckless individuals were treated as

This English portrait of Mataoka —better known as Pocahontas—may or may not actually resemble her. The Indian woman who married a Jamestown colonist and died in England remains a figure of mystery.

Ætatis suæ 21. Aº.1616.

human souvenirs, displayed as evidence of the strange lands visited by explorers. Often they were converted to Christianity and taught to speak English, French, or Spanish so that they could become interpreters. Many of these Native Americans were simply kidnapped. Even when they agreed to come, however, it is unlikely that they knew how far from their homes they would be taken.

Squanto, the Wampanoag who helped the Pilgrims, had been taken from his home in Patuxet (pah-TOOK-set), a village on Plymouth Bay, by trickery. He was one of about twenty Indians kidnapped by an English fishing captain in 1614. The captain took the Indians to Spain to sell them as slaves, but priests interfered with the sale. Historians do not know just what happened to Squanto, but a few years later he was living in London. He learned English and looked for someone to take him back to his home. When the Gorges expedition set out to establish a colony in New England in 1619, it took Squanto along as guide and interpreter.

Returning to Patuxet after an absence of five years, Squanto was not prepared for the devastation he found. His village had been completely wiped out—not by war, but by deadly disease epidemics that had swept along the coast, spreading sicknesses brought by the European visitors. It was not the only empty village. The Wampanoag population was greatly reduced, and Massasoit, the leader of

Pocahontas: Fact or Fiction? ❧

Pocahontas, the Indian princess who saved the life of one of the Jamestown settlers and later married another, is a romantic figure from early American history. Over the centuries, the story of her life has been embroidered with myths and guesswork. When they are stripped away, she remains a fascinating character who will always be something of a mystery.

Her real name was Mataoka. Pocahontas was a nickname that meant something like "naughty" or "playful." She was the daughter of Powhatan, chieftain of the Native American people of eastern Virginia. Pocahontas was around twelve or thirteen when the settlers arrived in Virginia. Soon afterward, she met John Smith, one of the Jamestown adventurers, at an Indian village. Legend says that Powhatan was going to kill Smith until Pocahontas pleaded with her father to spare the Englishman's life. That story was first recorded many years later, however, and it may not be true. If it is true, the event was almost certainly a ritual part of Smith's adoption into the Powhatan tribe, not a real danger. What is known is that Pocahontas helped carry food to Jamestown during the winter of 1607–1608.

Smith soon returned to England. Pocahontas married an Algonquin man and may have had a daughter. In 1612, after relations had soured between the settlers and the Indians, she was one of several Algonquin kidnapped and held hostage by the English. In 1614, while captive in Jamestown, she married a widowed settler named John Rolfe, who was launching the colony's tobacco industry. The marriage created an alliance between her tribe and the colony, but the alliance broke down when Powhatan, Pocahontas's father, died a couple of years later.

John and Rebecca Rolfe, as Pocahontas was known under her Christian name, had a son named Thomas. Soon after his birth, the family traveled to London so that Rolfe could arrange the sale of his tobacco. A few other members of Pocahontas's tribe went with them. London treated Pocahontas like a celebrity. She visited the court of King James I and had her portrait painted. But before the Rolfes could return to America, she became ill. She died in the Thames River port of Gravesend in 1616. John Rolfe sailed back to his tobacco farm but left Thomas in England under the care of his family. Among the many people who later traced their descent from this son of Pocahontas was Thomas Jefferson Randolph, grandson of Thomas Jefferson, the American president.

the survivors, was suspicious of the English. Massasoit did, however, send Squanto as his ambassador to the struggling Pilgrim colony in 1621. Squanto's help with farming and with making treaties with the neighboring Wampanoag communities probably saved the colony.

Alongside the hostility and suspicion that existed between Europeans and Native Americans, there was also curiosity, even fascination. To the Indians, the Europeans were a source of goods unlike any they had ever seen. Certain trade goods—especially metalware, alcohol, and guns—quickly became very desirable, and some tribes formed close trade alliances with various groups of Europeans. At the same time, some Europeans saw the Native American way of life as appealing. Expedition members and colonists occasionally went off to live with the Indians, sometimes to escape harsh conditions within their own communities. Even more surprising, some whites who were taken captive by Indian tribes refused to return to white society when they had the chance. This angered other whites, because it seemed to hint that maybe European life was not superior to Native American life after all.

Underlying all interactions between Europeans and Indians was a basic difference in the way they viewed the land. To the native peoples, it seemed obvious that the land was theirs. Land belonged to the community or tribe, not to individuals. If a tribe or chieftain chose to allow strangers from over the sea to build a village in Indian territory, that was one thing—but the strangers should not think that they had an absolute right to be there, especially in ever-growing numbers.

The Europeans, in contrast, came from a society in which individuals held deeds or titles that gave them the ownership or use of specific pieces of land. It was easy for them to convince themselves that the Indians, lacking this type of legal ownership, could or should be removed from the land. Europeans also claimed that land that was not being used should be available to anyone who wanted to build on it or farm it. They often refused to recognize Indian claims to large tracts of hunting territory.

Less than twenty years after the founding of the Plymouth colony, land caused a war between the Puritans and the Native Americans. By the 1630s, the Puritan colony was looking for room to expand. At the same time, the Pequot (PEH-kwat) tribe, which controlled the Connecticut River valley, was declining. The Puritans decided to take over Pequot territory and attacked the tribe in 1637. The biggest battle took place at an Indian fort on the Mystic River. The Puritans set fire to the fort and slaughtered the Pequot who tried to escape. They killed between 500 and 1,000 people, including men, women, and children.

Jamestown and Plymouth were just the beginning. The English wanted more of North America than a couple of tiny footholds on the edge of the continent. Their hunger for land would keep growing. As they started more colonies, conflict with the Indians continued to increase.

Honored as the "Protector and Preserver of the Pilgrims" on a statue near Plymouth Harbor, the Wampanoag chieftain Massasoit formed an alliance with the first English settlers in Massachusetts. Although he resisted the Pilgrims' attempts to turn his people into Christians, he took their side in conflicts with other Native Americans, and he gave them food during difficult times.

The massive masonry Castillo de San Marcos, the Spanish fort in St. Augustine, was completed in 1695.

CHAPTER SIX ❧
New Netherland, New France, and New Spain

ENGLAND SHARED NORTH AMERICA WITH other European powers during the period of exploration and colonization. France, the Netherlands, and Spain had colonies in what is now the United States. Each colony was unique, shaped by the goals and culture of its settlers and also by the geography and resources of its environment.

France Advances into the Interior

Jacques Cartier had opened the St. Lawrence River to French exploration in the mid-sixteenth century. His voyages had given France a territorial claim to Canada. Decades later, when France was ready to create a permanent colony in North America, Samuel de Champlain helped establish a settlement on the Canadian island of Nova Scotia. That colony did not last, but a few years later, in 1608, Champlain had better luck.

With a new royal monopoly on the fur trade, Champlain took settlers up the St. Lawrence River to the Huron Indian village of Stadacona, which Cartier had visited years before. Nearby, Champlain founded a settlement that he called Quebec, from the Huron name Kebec, which means "narrowing of the waters." It was not far from the site of Charlesbourg-Royal, the short-lived colony that Cartier had tried to establish half a century earlier. Cartier had failed, but

Founded by Samuel de Champlain on the site of the Indian town Stadacona, Quebec was the first significant French settlement in Canada. This image was made in 1761, two years after the city was taken by the British.

Champlain's new colony was successful. The French colonization of North America was under way.

In 1627, the crown reorganized the colony under the name New France. Champlain continued to be an important leader of the colony, but he spent much of his time exploring. Led by Indian guides, he found a large lake in what is now New York State; today it is known as Lake Champlain. Later Champlain traveled west to the far side of Lake Ontario. The geographic knowledge he gained during these expeditions, and the relationships he forged with Native American communities, were of immense help to the fur traders and missionaries who came after him. Champlain died in 1635. Although Quebec remained important after his death, the city of Montreal, founded farther up the river in 1642, took its place as the colony's base of exploration and trade.

From the start, French Canada was dominated by the fur trade. The northern woodlands and waterways were full of fur-bearing animals whose warm pelts were much desired by the hatmakers and coatmakers of Europe. Beaver pelts were especially prized, because they were waterproof. Roving colonists made their way into the interior to trap and hunt beaver and other animals, but the vast majority of the pelts were obtained through trade with the Native Americans.

Starting with Champlain, who recommended that travel up the St. Lawrence River past the rapids would be easier in native canoes rather than European-style boats, the French showed themselves quick to adopt practical elements of Native American culture. Over time, a number of fur traders took Indian wives, and a population of mixed-race people, the Métis (MAY-tees), emerged. Because New France was organized around trade rather than agriculture or ranching, its European population remained fairly small relative to its size, and the French did not immediately take control of large amounts of land. For all of these reasons, the French had generally good relations with the Indians—except for the powerful Iroquois tribes. The Iroquois people allied themselves with the English and eventually wiped out the Huron, who were the primary native allies of the French.

Like other European powers, the French considered it their duty to bring Christianity to the Indians. Roman Catholic missionaries were very active in New France. Often, they were the first Europeans to make contact with a new tribe or to travel a new route. Much of what modern historians know about New France comes from the chronicles of monks and priests like Jacques Marquette, who traveled down part of the Mississippi River with explorer Louis Joliet in 1673. A few years later, René-Robert Cavelier de La Salle traveled the length of the Mississippi and then established the second great center of French colonization in North America: the city of New Orleans, at the mouth of the Mississippi.

The French and English came into conflict in North America as early as 1621, when both nations claimed control of Nova Scotia. More often, though, it was fighting between the two nations in Europe that led to conflict between their colonists in America. The whole colonial era would be marked by a stream of wars between the French and the English.

The Dutch Claim

As the English were struggling to survive at Jamestown and the French were building Quebec, a new European power made its first move in North America. The Dutch East India Company of the Netherlands was becoming deeply involved in trade with Southeast Asia by way of the long, perilous sea routes around Africa and South America. Like others before them, the Dutch dreamed of finding a shorter, easier passage to the Indies. They sent Henry Hudson to find it for them.

Hudson was an English navigator who had already made two voyages for an English trading company that financed his search for the long-sought sea passage to Asia. On one voyage, he had turned back when his crew threatened to mutiny—a problem he would face again, with tragic results.

In 1609 Hudson sailed for the Dutch. Instead of searching for a Northwest Passage through North America, he hoped to find a Northeast Passage to the Indies by sailing around the top of Europe. But when his ship, the *Half Moon*, rounded the northern tip of Norway and sailed into the frigid Barents Sea, his crew of English and Dutch sailors grew rebellious. Fearing mutiny, Hudson changed course.

By 1650 about 50,000 people—Europeans and Africans—lived in the British North American colonies. The Spanish, Dutch, and French populations were smaller. Settlements were limited to the coast and along the St. Lawrence River. Most of the continent still belonged to the Native Americans.

ALGONQUIN
Quebec
ABENAKI
Lake Superior
CHIPPEWA
Montreal
Pemaquid
HURON
MOHAWK
Salem
CHIPPEWA
ONONDAGA
Boston
Fort Orange
IROQUOIS
CAYUGA
Lake Ontario
Hartford   Providence
Plymouth
OTTAWA
SENECA
NARRAGANSETT
PEQUOT
Lake Erie
ERIE
ONEIDA
New Haven
POTAWATOMI
New Netherland
SUSQUEHANNOCK
LENNI LENAPE (DELAWARE)
Ohio River
St. Mary's
SHAWNEE
POWHATAN
James River
Jamestown
TUSCARORA
CHEROKEE
ATLANTIC OCEAN
CHICKASAW
YAMASEE
CREEK
St. Augustine
Gulf of Mexico

Lake Michigan
St. Lawrence River
Connecticut River
Hudson River
Delaware River

	Spanish
	English
	French
	Dutch

0   100   200 Miles
0   100   200 Kilometers

NEW NETHERLAND, NEW FRANCE, AND NEW SPAIN   81

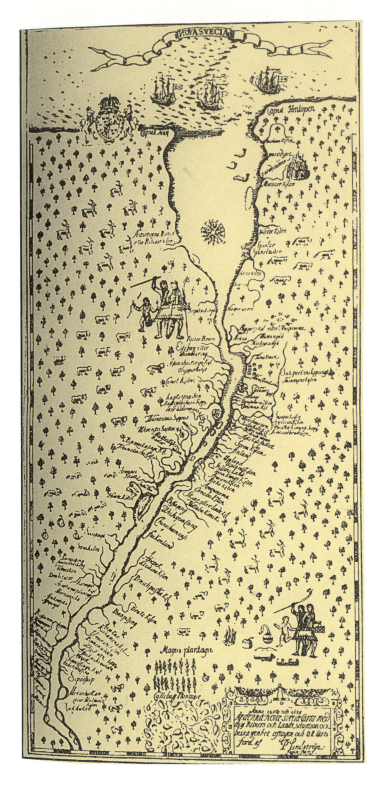

He returned to milder waters and crossed the Atlantic to North America. After sailing back and forth from Maine to the Chesapeake, he entered the bay, now known as the New York Bay, that Verrazano had found eighty-five years earlier. Perhaps, thought Hudson, he had found the Northwest Passage at last.

After several days of exploring the bay and trading with the local Indians for tobacco, food, and oysters, the expedition sailed farther into the bay, past Manhattan Island, and up a river. About 150 miles (240 kilometers) from the bay, near the present site of Albany, New York, Hudson anchored. A boatful of men went upriver to survey the course. Soon they returned with the disappointing news that the river grew small and shallow. It could not be the Northwest Passage. Hudson returned to his home in England and sent a report to the Dutch East India Company. His journey up the waterway that is

A 1654 map of New Sweden, a Scandinavian colony along the Delaware River. It passed into Dutch hands, and later became part of the British colonies.

The Norse Return to America ❧

Norse Vikings from Scandinavia had pioneered the way to Vinland 500 years before Columbus. A century and a half after Columbus, Scandinavians planted a new colony in North America.

Swedish, German, and Dutch investors formed a trading company to set up a colony on the Delaware River. As their leader they chose Peter Minuit, who had been the director of New Netherland for five years. He knew colonial geography and had experience in dealing with Native Americans.

The company's ships arrived in America in 1638. At the site of present-day Wilmington, Delaware, the colonists built Fort Christina, the first permanent European settlement along the river. Over the next few years, about 600 Swedish and Finnish colonists arrived in New Sweden. Their forts and farms dotted the river's banks from present-day Maryland to New Jersey. In 1565, after New Sweden and New Netherland clashed over ownership of a fort, the Dutch colony sent armed ships and soldiers to New Sweden. The Scandinavian settlers surrendered peacefully to New Netherland, which let them remain largely independent. Later they were absorbed into the English colonies that took root along the Delaware.

now called the Hudson River became the basis for a Dutch territorial claim to the bay of New York and everything around it, as well as the Hudson River valley.

Hudson made a fourth voyage, this time seeking the Northwest Passage in the Canadian Arctic on behalf of a group of English merchants. He entered a vast bay, as big as a sea, and began probing its coast for a westward passage. When Hudson made it clear that he planned to spend the winter there so that he could keep looking for the passage the following summer, his crewmen feared that his plan meant death for all of them. They mutinied and set the captain, his son, and six loyal followers adrift in a small boat, leaving them to die on the cold, lonely waters of Hudson Bay.

The Dutch lost no time in acting on the claim Hudson had made for them. In 1614 they built a fur-trading post on the Hudson River, at the spot where Albany stands today. That site became known as Fort Orange. Seven years later, they organized the Dutch West India Company to establish a colony and, they hoped, make a profit from it.

The colony of New Netherland was founded in 1624, when the company sent thirty families to Manhattan Island. They established a settlement at the island's southern tip. In 1626 an officer of the company bought the entire island from the local Native Americans—or so he thought. The Indians probably thought they were only agreeing to let the Dutch rent or use the land. At any rate, the colonists set about building a walled community they called New Amsterdam. They built practical structures geared toward commerce and economy. In addition to houses and a fort, there was a sturdy countinghouse (a place to keep money and trade goods) and a flour mill that they also used as a church.

Henry Hudson, who explored for the Dutch East India Company, survived several near mutinies before being set adrift in a small boat, with his son and a few followers, in the cold waters of Hudson Bay. No trace of them has ever been found.

New Netherland's most distinctive feature was the diversity of its population. Because the parent country, the Netherlands, was fairly prosperous and religiously tolerant, there was no specific group of Dutch people eager to leave their homeland for a remote frontier colony. Although some Dutch people did settle in the colony, New Netherland received settlers from all over northern and western Europe. It welcomed Jews at a time when some countries were persecuting them. Native Americans lived in the colony as well, some as slaves and others as free people. In addition, the Dutch—who were active in the slave trade at an early date—quickly imported black slaves to New Netherland from Africa, the Caribbean, and South America. In

1642 a resident of this multicultural community wrote that he could hear eighteen languages spoken in New Amsterdam.

In spite of its variety, the colony's population remained small. By 1643 it had fewer than 2,000 people. Some of them farmed along the Hudson River, where wealthy landowners called patroons (pat-ROONS) had large estates. Other New Netherlanders were engaged in trade, chiefly with the Iroquois peoples. Still, the colony never be-

The Dutch settlement of New Amsterdam was a sturdily built, multi-cultural trading port. After it surrendered to the English in 1664, its name was changed to New York.

came the busy, profitable enterprise that its founders had imagined. The Dutch West India Company, busy with larger trade operations in places like Brazil and Africa, let New Netherland grow at a slow pace.

In 1652 the Dutch and English went to war in Europe and on the high seas. New Netherland played no part in this war, but when a second conflict broke out in the mid-1660s, English warships appeared off New Amsterdam. With no military defense force, and no desire to have their town attacked and destroyed, the colonists surrendered to the English in 1664. New Netherland eventually became an English colony, and its name was changed to New York. Many residents of New Netherland and New Amsterdam stayed on after the colony changed hands. They gave the Hudson River valley a definite Dutch flavor, and they helped make New York one of the most culturally diverse towns in the English colonies.

The Spanish Borderlands

Spain, the first of the European powers to colonize the Americas, eventually controlled most of South America, all of Central America, and part of North America. In 1535 the Spanish crown organized the North American territory into a colony called the viceroyalty of New Spain. Its top administrator, the viceroy, was the personal representative of the crown.

New Spain sprawled across part of Central America, all of Mexico, Cuba, and the other Spanish possessions in the Caribbean, and two regions that were known as the Spanish Borderlands, because they formed the northern border of Spain's territory. Both of the Spanish Borderlands lay inside the present-day boundary of the United States. One of them was Florida. The other was a gigantic section of the Southwest, from Texas to California.

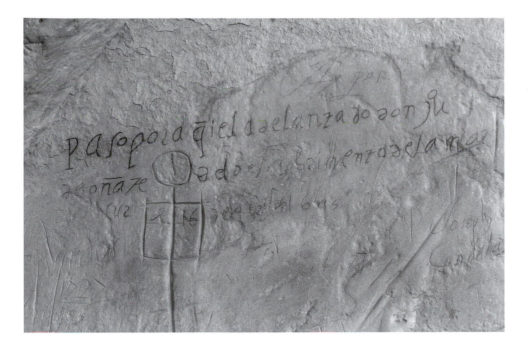

During an exploring expedition into the Southwest, conquistador Juan de Oñate carved an inscription into a sandstone bluff at what is now El Morro, New Mexico.

The capital of New Spain was Mexico City, which Cortés had seized from the Aztec. At the time when the English were hammering together their first huts at Jamestown, Mexico City had a huge cathedral, a university, and a publishing house. The city was the chief seat of government and economic activity in the colony. Officials there oversaw the administration of the Borderlands.

Spain had claimed Florida since the 1513 expedition of Ponce de León, but it took a closer interest in the territory after French Huguenots tried to settle there in the 1560s. The Spanish got rid of the Huguenots. Then they fortified St. Augustine and started keeping soldiers in Florida to defend the territory. Spain also built a monastery in St. Augustine and increased its missionary activity in Florida. By the 1630s, there were forty-four missions in Florida. Most were on the Atlantic coast or in the north. At these settlements, monks and priests worked to convert the Indians to Christianity.

Aside from the soldiers and the monks, however, Spain sent relatively few settlers to Florida. This particular Spanish Borderland would later come under English control.

Pedro Menéndez de Avilés, a poor Spanish nobleman who became a renowned sea captain, was hired by King Philip II to colonize Florida for Spain. He founded St. Augustine in 1565, after destroying a French Protestant colony that had taken root in Florida the previous year.

Coronado's expedition had explored the area far north of Mexico in the mid-fifteenth century, but the conquistador had failed to find any sources of gold or silver. Later, a series of expeditions opened up northern Mexico to settlement and exploitation. Then, at the end of the sixteenth century, a wealthy and influential colonist, an immigrant from Spain who had married a great-granddaughter of the last Aztec emperor, financed an expedition north of Mexico. His name was Juan de Oñate. He led a party of about 400 soldiers, adventurers, and priests into a territory that he named New Mexico. Oñate claimed this region for Spain and became its governor.

Like Coronado, Oñate hoped to find legendary cities of gold somewhere in the interior. Instead, he created a new city of his own—or rather, a small settlement he called San Juan de los Caballeros. Oñate had offered the local Indian tribes peace, if they agreed to submit to his government and to accept Christianity. They agreed, but the relationship was hostile from the start. After the Acoma killed

A Survivor's Story ⌘

Álvar Núñez Cabeza de Vaca was one of a handful of Spanish adventurers who survived a disastrous shipwreck on the coast of Texas in 1528. Eight years later, Cabeza de Vaca and three comrades turned up in New Spain. They had experienced enslavement, hunger, disease, and a long and difficult journey on foot. Cabeza de Vaca wrote an account of his travels through eastern Texas and north-eastern Mexico. In addition to being an astonishing adventure story, his tale is packed with information about geography, plant and animal life, and Native Americans, including this description of a desolate region:

We travelled over a great part of the country, and found it all deserted, as the people had fled to the mountains, leaving houses and fields out of fear of the Christians. This filled our hearts with sorrow, seeing the land so fertile and beautiful, so full of water and streams, but abandoned and the places burned down, and the people, so thin and wan, fleeing and hiding; and as they did not raise any crops their destitution had become so great that they ate tree-bark and roots. . . . They brought us blankets, which they had concealed from the Christians, and gave them to us, and told how the Christians had penetrated into the country before, and had destroyed and burnt the villages, taking with them half the men and all the women and children, and how those who could escaped by flight.

Oñate's nephew in a surprise attack, he launched a short, brutal war against them. His forces swarmed through the Acoma pueblo, killing 500 men and 300 women and children. Hundreds more women and children stood trial and endured punishment. Those who survived had to serve twenty years as servants.

After putting down the Acoma rebellion, Oñate continued exploring the Borderlands, ranging from Kansas to the Gulf of California. He failed to find any source of wealth, however, and some of the New Mexico colonists grew discontented with his governorship.

When word of trouble in New Mexico reached the viceroy in Mexico City, Oñate was called to the capital to be tried for a variety of crimes, including inhumane cruelty against the Indians. He spent seven years and all his fortune defending himself from the charges. Finally, he went to Spain, where he eventually received a pardon from the king. He never returned to New Mexico.

By the early years of the seventeenth century, the colonization of North America by the European powers was well under way. Spain, France, England, and the Netherlands had established settlements that would endure and grow, anchoring other, newer forts, villages, and towns. Although Spanish influence had spread throughout Mexico and the French had ventured inland along the St. Lawrence River, most of the first colonies clung to the coasts. Ship traffic maintained vitally important lines of supply, providing colonists with food and other necessities from their home countries.

In the years ahead, explorers would probe the far north, the Pacific coast, and the interior, slowly filling in more of the blank spaces on the map of North America. At the same time, the Europeans who lived in the first small colonies would face the daily challenges of adapting to life in a new continent. They would learn to produce at least some of what they needed, and then, moving beyond mere survival, they would begin to create communities, economies, and governments. These colonists' lives would be shaped in part by hardship and conflict, and their growing presence would bring hardship and conflict in turn to the Native Americans, descendants of the continent's first colonizers.

Timeline ❧

Before 10000 B.C.E.	The first people reach the Americas.
Around 1000 C.E.	Leif Eiriksson and other Vikings explore North America's coast.
1492	Christopher Columbus tries to sail from Spain to China but finds the Americas.
1496	Spain founds the settlement of Santo Domingo on Hispaniola.
1497	John Cabot reaches the coast of North America.
1513	Ponce de Léon explores and claims Florida.
1524	Giovanni da Verrazano, exploring for France, travels along the coast of North America.
1531	From its colony in Mexico, Spain begins exploring the Southwest.
1534–1542	French explorer Jacques Cartier makes several voyages into Canada; in 1541 he establishes the settlement of Charlesbourg-Royal.
1539–1542	Hernando de Soto leads a band of conquistadors through the Southeast.
1540–1542	Francisco Vásquez de Coronado explores the Southwest and finds the Grand Canyon.
1565	Spain establishes St. Augustine, Florida, the oldest continuously lived-in city in the present-day United States.
1579	English navigator Francis Drake reaches the California coast.
1584–1586	England tries to establish a colony at Roanoke, Virginia.
1595	The Spanish crown gives Juan de Oñate permission to colonize New Mexico.
1607	England establishes its first permanent American colony at Jamestown, Virginia.
1608	Samuel de Champlain founds the French colony of Quebec in Canada.
1609	Henry Hudson's voyage gives the Dutch a claim to New York.
1614	The Dutch build a trading post on the Hudson River.
1619	Jamestown imports twenty African slaves.
1620	English Puritans, called Pilgrims, settle at Plymouth, Massachusetts.
1624	Dutch families begin to settle in New Netherland.

Glossary ❧

anthropologist	Scientist who studies the similarities and differences among various human cultures.
archaeologist	Scientist who studies past cultures and civilizations, usually by examining physical traces such as ruins and objects left behind.
Black Death	Name given by Europeans to the bubonic plague, a disease that killed huge numbers of people in repeated epidemics.
Clovis culture	A culture established by about 11,500 years ago in what is now the southwestern United States; first identified by stone tools and other objects found at Clovis, New Mexico.
conquistador	Spanish military explorer who participated in the exploration and conquest of the Americas.
courtier	Member of a king's or queen's court.
fool's gold	Iron pyrite, a mineral that is often mistaken for gold.
geologist	Scientist who studies the physical structure of the earth, past and present.
glaciation	Period during an ice age when large ice sheets form over land and sea.
Huguenots	French Protestants.
missionary	Someone who works to convert people to a new religion.
Northwest Passage	Geographers' and explorers' fantasy of an easy-to-navigate water route through or around North America that would link the Atlantic and Pacific oceans; does not exist.
Paleo-Indians	Early peoples in the Americas; ancestors of the Native Americans. The links between Paleo-Indians and modern Indians are not clear.
peninsula	Arm of land that sticks out into a body of water.
pueblo	Village; used in the Southwest to refer to both Native American and Spanish communities.
Puritan	A Protestant in sixteenth- or seventeenth-century England who wanted to purify, or reform, the church.
Sanguenay	Imaginary kingdom in the interior of Canada that was described to European explorers by Indians.
Seafaring	Traveling by sea; can describe a people or nation that makes effective use of ships or boats.
Skraelings	Norse name for the Native American peoples of Greenland and eastern Canada.
Spanish Borderlands	Parts of the Spanish North American territories that were north of the Mexican colony.

Primary Source List ✍

Chapter 2   **p. 23**   Bjarni Herjolfsson from *The Greenlanders' Saga*. In *The Norse Atlantic Saga*, by Gwyn Jones. New York: Oxford University Press, 1964.

                 p. 31   Christopher Columbus from "Columbus's Letter Announcing His Discoveries in the New World (1493)." In *Colonial America: An Encyclopedia of Social, Political, Cultural, and Economic History*, ed. James Ciment. Vol. 5. Armonk, NY: M.E. Sharpe, 2006.

Chapter 3   **p. 45**   Bernal Diaz del Castillo from *The Discovery and Conquest of Mexico, 1517–1521*. New York: Da Capo, 2003.

                 p. 47   Bartolomé de Las Casas from *A Brief Account of the Devastation of the Indies*. 1552. Online at www.historyisaweapon.com/defcon1/delascasas.html.

Chapter 4   **p. 50**   Lorenzo Pasqualigo from "John Cabot's Discovery of North America (1497)." In *Colonial America: An Encyclopedia of Social, Political, Cultural, and Economic History*, ed. James Ciment. Vol. 5. Armonk, NY: M.E. Sharpe, 2006.

Chapter 5   **p. 70**   Edward Winslow from "A Relation or Journal of the Proceedings of the Plantation Settled at Plymouth in New England." In *1491: New Revelations of the Americas Before Columbus*, by Charles A. Mann. New York: Knopf, 2005.

Chapter 6   **p. 89**   Álvar Núñez Cabeza de Vaca from *The Journey of Álvar Núñez Cabeza de Vaca*, ed. Adolph F. Bandalier. New York: Barnes, 1905. Available online at www.americanjourneys.org/aj-070/index.asp.

For More Information ✑

The books and Web sites listed below contain information about the exploration and early settlement of North America. Most of the books were written especially for young adults. The others will not be too difficult for most young readers. The Web site addresses were accurate when this book was written, but remember that sites and their addresses change frequently. Your librarian can help you find additional resources.

Books

Ciment, James, ed. *Colonial America: An Encyclopedia of Social, Political, Cultural, and Economic History.* Armonk, NY: M.E. Sharpe, 2006.

Faber, Harold. *The Discoverers of America.* New York: Scribner, 1992.

————. *La Salle: Down the Mississippi.* New York: Benchmark Books, 2002.

Hakim, Joy. *The First Americans.* New York: Oxford University Press, 2003.

Podell, Janet, and Steven Anzovin. *Old Worlds to New: The Age of Exploration and Discovery.* New York: Wilson, 1993.

Rossi, Ann. *Cultures Collide: Native Americans and Europeans, 1492–1700.* Washington, DC: National Geographic, 2004.

Saffer, Barbara. *Henry Hudson: Ill-Fated Explorer of North America's Coast.* Philadelphia: Chelsea House, 2002.

Shields, Charles J. *John Cabot and the Rediscovery of North America.* Philadelphia: Chelsea House, 2002.

Stefoff, Rebecca. *Exploring the New World.* Tarrytown, NY: Benchmark Books, 2001.

Waldman, Stuart. *We Asked for Nothing: The Remarkable Journey of Cabeza de Vaca.* New York: Mikaya, 2003.

Wilbur, C. Keith. *Early Explorers of North America.* Philadelphia: Chelsea House, 1997.

Web Sites

www.sfu.museum/journey

An overview of current theories and evidence about the peopling of the Americas, created by the Museum of Archaeology and Ethnology of Canada's Simon Fraser University.

www.infoplease.com/ipa/A0002130.htm

A timeline of the Native American cultures that developed in North America before Christopher Columbus's arrival.

www.americanjourneys.org

A digital library of more than 18,000 pages of original documents about the exploration and settlement of North America, in an easy-to-use site maintained by the Wisconsin Historical Society and funded by the U.S. Institute of Museum and Library Services.

www.cdli.ca/CITE/explorer.htm

Biographies and other information about the Europeans who explored North America.

www.ibiblio.org/expo/1492.exhibit/Intro.html

The Library of Congress's "1492: An Ongoing Voyage" site explores the background, events, and lingering effects of Columbus's historic journeys.

www.apva.org/jr.html

The Jamestown Rediscovery site of the Association for the Preservation of Virginia Antiquities has a brief history of the Jamestown colony, as well as information about archaeological work at the location today.

Index 🙰

Note: Page numbers in italics refer to pictures and maps.